Shipwreck Sagas

Gary Gentile

Bellerophon Bookworks

Bellerophon Bookworks
P.O. Box 57137
Philadelphia, PA 19111

Additional copies of this book may be purchased from the same address by sending a check or money order in the amount of $20 U.S. for each copy (plus $4 shipping per order, not per book). For information about consulting services, workshops, presentations, and a list of available titles that can be ordered online and paid by credit card, visit the GGP website:

http://www.ggentile.com

All uncredited photographs were taken by the author. Front cover: six-inch fossil shark tooth, china and ladle inside the *P.L.M. 27*, bell from the *Sebastian*, helm stand from the *Miraflores*, gauges inside the *President Coolidge*. Back cover: bell on the *Bow Mariner*, sand tiger shark, ladder on the *P.L.M. 27*, china inside the *President Coolidge*, porthole inside the *Manuela.*

International Standard Book Numbers (ISBN)
1-883056-34-9
978-1-883056-34-6

First Edition

Printed in the U.S.A.

Contents

Shipwreck Sagas is a collection of my shorter works. Most have seen print in books, magazines, newspapers, or on the Internet. Some I have expanded for this collection because space limitations in the original publication precluded me from telling the story in its entirety. Others I have let stand the way they were published, but I have appended annotations either beforehand or afterward.

The wreck sagas in "Lost Chapters from Shipwrecks of New York" are published here for the first time. I wrote "The Wreck of the Granny" exclusively for inclusion in this volume.

By Way of Biography

I was certified for scuba in 1970. I started diving on New Jersey shipwrecks the following year. I bought my first drysuit in 1972. I had to, because I was shivering so hard in my wetsuit that my teeth chattered on the mouthpiece of my regulator, and my body parts were close to spinning away in the cold New Jersey sea like parts of a broken flywheel.

The drysuit was called a Unisuit. It was manufactured by the Norwegian company Poseidon, which had just started distributing its product in the United States. The drysuit was made of quarter-inch neoprene. The material was so thick and stiff that diving in it was a workout. Moving my arms and legs was like doing isometrics.

Worse than the inflexibility, the drysuit soon commenced to leak like a sieve. These leaks occurred mostly at the seams, where they were nearly impossible to patch. I owned three Unisuits during the next eight years: a black one, a blue one, and a red one. The change in color did not reduce the drysuit's potential for leakage.

Another disadvantage was the watertight zipper. The zipper started between the shoulder blades, then went down the back, between the legs, and up along the belly to the sternum. The drysuit was designed for commercial divers who had to live in the suit for an entire shift. The zipper design allowed them to take care of bodily functions without having to completely remove the suit, or unseal the cuffs an neck seal.

Unless one had the arms of a contortionist or an orangutan, the zipper could not be pulled down or up the back without help. Worse, because of the stress that was placed upon the zipper in the curvature of the crotch, the teeth soon separated the slightest amount. A leak developed in the most sensitive area. I used to hate the incursion of frigid water on my testicles. This type of leak was not repairable.

I also bought a Viking drysuit. The rubberized canvas was extremely pliable, and the seams never leaked. While this might "seam" like a dream come true, there were problems which, while not insurmountable, were at the very least somewhat inconvenient.

The Viking suit could not leak at the zipper because it didn't have one. Entry was made through the neck seal. You read right: I had to stretch the latex neck seal wide enough to get my entire body through the opening. The instruction manual stated that a diver could do this by himself, but I could never get the hang of it.

I could pull the neck seal over my legs, waist, and lower abdomen, right up to my armpits. Then I was stuck. It took at least one person and sometimes two people to pull apart the neck seal so I could get my arms through it one at a time. I also needed one or two people to help me to get out of the drysuit.

Climbing into the Viking drysuit was like squeezing into a giant condom. Peeling off the drysuit was like squirming through the birth canal into the cruel outer world.

A second disadvantage was the poor insulating quality of the material. In those days, before the development of snowmobile suits, there was no way that I could stay warm in cold water, even with expedition weight long johns.

Eventually I relegated the Viking drysuit to winter whitewater canoeing. It worked admirably for this purpose. When I tried paddling in my Unisuit, the muscles in my arms became exhausted after a couple of miles, and I worked up a sweat. The Viking suit was perfect: extremely flexible and durable, and it didn't leak. This was a godsend, for example, when I swamped in a big rapid on the Lehigh River during a snowstorm in late December, and had to swim for half a mile before I could drag my canoe onto a boulder.

The worst part about that trip was the subfreezing temperature of the air. Water that sloshed over the gunwales quickly turned to slush, then to ice. My legs froze to the bottom of the boat. I chipped away the ice with the blade of my paddle, else I would have drowned if the canoe overturned. Thereafter I continually moved my legs in order to keep them free.

My only companion on this trip was Walt Hauser. He was paddling a kayak. He started complaining that something was blocking his vision. When I looked at him, I saw that a three-inch icicle was growing down between his eyes from the brim of his helmet, like the noseguard worn by the jousting knights of yesteryear.

In 1980, I heard about a new drysuit that had entered the marketplace. The CF-200 was made by Diving Unlimited International. The acronym is DUI, pronounced as individual letters, but I always pronounce it like one of Donald Duck's three nephews: Dewey.

In one fell swoop, the DUI suit resolved all the problems that plagued the Unisuit and the Viking suit. The material was crushed neoprene: that is, quarter-inch neoprene that had the air bubbles crushed out of it. This made the suit both durable and flexible.

The zipper ran diagonally across the chest from the upper left shoulder to the right hip. The placement made the suit both self-donning and self-doffing. Because no stress was placed on the zipper, it didn't bulge and cause the teeth to separate.

DUI offered a one-piece heavy-duty Thinsulate undergarment that could be worn over long johns for extra warmth.

I bought a DUI suit right away, and I have worn DUI suits exclusively ever since.

After twelve years of hard wear, the drysuit was looking pretty ragged. The original bright orange panels had been sunbaked to a dull finish. The surface was pockmarked with dollops of neoprene cement and AquaSeal, where I had patched puncture wounds that I had accumulated from bumping against barnacles and the sharp metal edges of hull plates. The kneepads had

Val Askins took this picture of me on a trip to the *Andrea Doria* in 2004.

been completely destroyed from crawling over rocks on shore dives. And the outer lining was badly delaminating, peeling off in sheets so as to make me look like Boris Karloff's mummy, whose wrappings had become unraveled.

Dick Long, DUI founder and owner, thought that as a highly visible figure in the diving community, the decrepit drysuit did not do me justice - nor did it advertise DUI suits the way Dick wanted them to be perceived. He made me an offer that I couldn't refuse.

He offered to give me a new DUI suit in exchange for my old one, which he could use for advertising purposes, as a testimonial to the suit's endurance. I agreed.

I was shocked when I first saw my old drysuit on display at a diving conference. It was hung next to a sign that read something like, "This drysuit was worn by Gary Gentile for twelve years."

I have bought two DUI suits since. I rotate them, so I always have a backup when one needs to be sent to the factory for repair.

In 2008, after Dick took me on a private tour of the DUI facility in San Diego, Faith Ortins, Vice President of Sales, asked me to write a biographical piece for the DUI website. She posed the questions; I wrote my answers.

DUI Questionnaire

When / where did you start diving?

I was certified in Philadelphia in 1970.

What motivated you to become a diver?

I used to do a lot of spelunking (cave exploring), some in Pennsylvania but most in Virginia and West Virginia. The grotto that changed my life was Blue Hole, Virginia. The entrance was a sinkhole at the bottom of which flowed an underground river. I lowered an inflatable raft 90 feet down to the water level, then climbed down a rope into the raft. I convinced two friends to go with me.

We paddled along this subterranean passageway, and explored some side passageways that were dry. Half a mile from the entrance, the rocky roof dipped down to the surface of the river, blocking further exploration. The water was crystal clear and 50 feet deep. I figured that if I took a diving course, I could return to Blue Hole and explore the submerged portion of the passageway, and hopefully discover an air pocket on the other side.

Immediately upon my return home, I called the YMCA and signed up for diving lessons. After I was certified, I was never able to convince anyone to lower dive gear 90 feet down into the river. I never got to explore the other side of the submerged passageway. In the meantime I discovered wreck-diving.

Where have you been?

I was an infantryman in Vietnam. I have skied in Austria, Colorado, Quebec, and all the States in the northeast quadrant (except for Connecticut). I have done a great deal of backpacking and mountain climbing in Pennsylvania, New England, the western States (Arizona, California, Colorado, New Mexico, Utah, South Dakota, and Washington, among others), and once in Australia. Except for one trip down the Rio Grande in Texas, and another down the St. John River in Maine, all my wilderness canoeing trips took place in Canada (Labrador, Quebec, Ontario, and the Northwest Territories).

I have dived off every State along the American eastern seaboard, from Newfoundland and Nova Scotia to the Dry Tortugas. I have dived in all five Great Lakes. I have also dived off England, Ireland, Scotland, Australia, Vanuatu, and off a number of islands in the Caribbean, plus Bermuda. Recently I dived off San Diego, California.

What diving accomplishment are you most proud of?

The *Monitor*. More important than the dive was winning the suit against NOAA and the federal government. This case not only cleared the way for future generations to dive on the site of the Civil War ironclad, but established the precedent that American citizens do not have to abide by NOAA regulations with regard depth. Although NOAA divers are not permitted to dive deeper than 130 feet, non-NOAA divers may dive as deep as they want.

What will the sport of diving be like 20 years from now?

I speculate that tank diving will yield to rebreather diving.

Who do you admire in the diving community?

Everyone who carries the torch of human progress another step farther.

Do you have any pre-dive, dive, or deco rituals?

I always spit into my mask, I breathe slowly and deeply, and I blow air rings to pass the time.

Do you have any advice for a new drysuit diver?
Try it. You won't like it – you'll *love* it.

Do you know any good dive / fish jokes?
More than you want to hear. They're all groaners and bad puns (or so people tell me; I think they're clever).

Where can people find out more about you, your courses, and products?
On my website: http://www.ggentile.com. A brief biography is on the home page. Of my 51 book titles, those that are presently in print can be viewed on different screens. *The Lusitania Controversies* contains the complete history of wreck-diving, including my participation in the activity. Also included is a real-life account of my combat service in Vietnam. *Lonely Conflict* is a novelized autobiography of my military service.

With respect to diving accomplishments, I refrained from mentioning the Ostfriesland*: the German battleship that was sunk by Billy Mitchell's bombers in 1921. It lies at a depth of 380 feet. Ken Clayton, Pete Manchee, and I dived on this wreck in 1990, breathing a mixture of heliox that consisted of 12% oxygen and 88% helium.*

This seminal dive, and the write-ups about it, provided the primary stimulus for the advent of mixed-gas and technical diving. I thought that despite the truth of the matter, citing this fact might sound vain.

I am always being asked, "What is your favorite shipwreck?" My stock answer is that I don't have one particular favorite, but I have a "top ten" list of those that I have found the most visually impressive, exciting to explore, or historically significant.

Six of these wrecks are covered in the present volume. I covered the Lusitania *and the* Monitor *in* Shipwreck Heresies. *I covered the* San Diego *and the* Wilkes-Barre *in* Wreck Diving Adventures.

I have written books about four of the wrecks on my "top ten" list: two books on the Andrea Doria, *two books on the* Lusitania, *one book on the* Monitor, *and one book on the* San Diego.

In alphabetical order, my top ten favorite wrecks are:

Andrea Doria
Dunderberg
Empress of Ireland
Florida
Lusitania
Monitor
Ostfriesland
President Coolidge
San Diego
Wilkes-Barre

A postcard picture of the *Andrea Doria* passing the Rock of Gibraltar.

Top Ten Tech Wrecks

As a follow-up to the previous page on which I listed my top ten favorite shipwrecks, one magazine editor asked me to write a sidebar about my top ten favorite technical wrecks. I have listed them from shallowest to deepest.

You might think that I should have included the President Coolidge, *which reaches a maximum depth of 240 feet. I had not yet dived on the* Coolidge *at the time I wrote this piece. And anyway, because the bow is accessible from shore at a depth of 55 feet, and is dived most often by single-tank divers, it is difficult to think of it as a true technical wreck.*

Five of these wrecks overlap by also appearing in my "top ten" favorites.

Name: *Coimbra*
Location: south shore of Long Island, New York
Depth: 180 feet, rising to 150 feet
Conditions: generally clear with little or no current; nets and monofilament minimal.
Comments: a great technical training dive because it is deep yet not overly so, a bit forgiving due to normally good conditions, and accessible by many charter boats.
Certifications required: deep air.

Coimbra. (Official U.S. Coast Guard photo.)

Choapa. (Official U.S. Coast Guard photo.)

Name: *Choapa*
Location: the Mud Hole, off northern New Jersey.
Depth: 200 feet, rising to 170 feet.
Conditions: generally so dark as to constitute a night dive, silting a serious threat, totally enshrouded in nets and monofilament (a two-knife dive - some say three), powerful backup lights a necessity, a well-trained buddy a godsend.
Comments: just because you have dived on the *Andrea Doria* does not mean that you are ready for the *Choapa*; not as deep, but certainly more dangerous. Nearby *Ioannis P. Goulandris* is a little brighter and harbors fewer nets and strands of monofilament; both wrecks lie basically upright but with gaping rust holes and large areas of collapse.
Certifications required: deep air; mixed gas may be more of a liability due to the potential for side-slung decompression bottles to become entangled in monofilament.

Name: *Monitor*
Location: Cape Hatteras, North Carolina
Depth: 230 feet, rises to 215 feet
Conditions: extremely variable with stark transformations occurring overnight, depending upon the position of the Gulf Stream; current ranges from zero to ripping and is generally strong, with the ever present possibility of a dive being aborted; visibility can be zero or more than 100 feet, but averages 50 to 75 feet; white sandy bottom with high reflectivity.
Comments: straightforward dive under the best condi-

tions because the wreck is small and exposed; cyclical currents prevent silt accumulation; no fishing allowed on site, so nets and monofilament are seldom seen; due to strong currents, decompression is best done adrift, which necessitates establishing a breakaway system with a free-floating decompression station.

Certifications required: deep air for those with high tolerance to narcosis; otherwise, mixed gas.

Monitor. (Courtesy of the Naval Photographic Center.)

Name: *Andrea Doria*

Location: 55 miles south of Nantucket Island, Massachusetts.

Depth: 240 feet, rises to 195 feet (used to rise to 165).

Conditions: potentially high current and low ambient light, penetration readily accessible and therefore deceptively easy, nets and monofilament a constant hazard.

Comments: wreck lying on starboard side, hull partially intact, interior a maze of corridors and beckoning stairwells, loose wires and cables hanging about like snares for the unwary; because the wreck is so big and visibility is often limited (average 30 feet) it may be difficult to relocate the anchor line; disorientation inside is accentuated by the wreck's 90 degree list. Washouts at bow and stern go as deep as 250 feet.

Certifications required: deep air for exterior exploration of the high-side hull, mixed gas for penetration and for excursions to the seabed and the low-side hull.

Name: *Wilkes-Barre*
Location: Key West, Florida.
Depth: 250 feet; bow rises to 180 feet, stern to 155 feet.
Conditions: deceptively easy due to bright ambient light, but still deep; a good beginner "tech wreck" often used for training; visibility best when the Gulf Stream is in, but dive may be aborted by strong current.
Comments: wreck broken in two amidships: bow half lies on starboard side with the port hull rising to 180 feet, stern half rests on an even keel and bristles with guns and turrets which are visually spectacular, with the top of the stack reaching 155 feet; penetration readily accessible and therefore deceptively easy; despite ambient brightness, silting can reduce interior visibility to zero. One time I reached 260 feet by crawling under the keel and emerging on the other side. U.S. submarine *S-16* is nearby at the same depth, but with only a 20-foot rise.
Certifications required: deep air for upper levels; mixed gas for lower levels; penetration skills include re-attaching side-slung bottles which should be left outside entrance points.

Wilkes-Barre. (From the author's collection.)

The stern of the *Kamloops*.

Name: *Kamloops*
Location: Isle Royale, in Lake Superior.
Depth: 260 feet, rising to 180 feet.
Conditions: extremely cold with dark green water; no current or fishing lines.
Comments: drysuit necessary for long exposures as the temperature never gets more than 5° to 10° above freezing even in summer, although decompression depths may be warmer; hull intact lying on starboard side; stern rests high on a ledge, bow noses down into the mud; debris field fans out across a black mud and rock bottom which absorbs nearly all light; penetration possible; practically no current; gear washing unnecessary because the water is fresh and clean.
Certifications required: deep air for the high side; mixed gas for the low side and lakebed.

Name: *Washington*
Location: Cape Henry, Virginia.
Depth: 290 feet, rising to 250 feet.
Conditions: bright clear water with a white sandy bottom and little current.
Comments: capsized U.S. battleship with hull intact except at the sand level; difficult to grapple because the hull plates are unbroken and no rust holes are evident. Ambient light on the bottom can be so bright that a dive light is useless.

Washington under construction. (Courtesy of the National Archives.)

Certifications required: although I breathed air on this wreck, I recommend mixed gas for greater clarity of mind.

Name: *Lusitania*
Location: southwest corner of Ireland.
Depth: 310 feet
Conditions: dark enough to be considered a night dive under most circumstances; visibility affected by floating plankton, and ranges from 8 feet to 30 feet; nets everywhere and extremely hazardous; temperature tolerable; location tidal.
Comments: superstructure gone, hull listing to starboard in an advanced degree of collapse and deterioration; line reel usage advised for explorations out of sight of the descent line; because the tides are so strong, dives can be made only during slack, and decompression must be conducted on a floating station secured to the descent line with a breakaway system.
Certifications required: mixed gas.

Lusitania. (From the author's collection.)

New Jersey. (Courtesy of the National Archives.)

Name: *New Jersey*
Location: Diamond Shoals, North Carolina
Depth: 330 feet, rising to 290.
Conditions: usually clear Gulf Stream water which may exert a considerable current.
Comments: capsized U.S. battleship with the hull intact and unbroken; visibility good; capsized sister ship *Virginia* lies one mile offshore at a depth of 350 feet; grappling difficult.
Certifications required: mixed gas.

Name: *Ostfriesland*
Location: Cape Charles, Virginia.
Depth: 380 feet, rising to 320 feet.
Conditions: current a possibility, temperature reasonable, visibility good but dark; most daunting feature is the extreme depth.
Comments: German battleship lying upside down; the focal point of seven other German warships scuttled within a several mile radius during aerial bombing tests conducted in 1921; cruiser *Frankfurt* lies upright at 420 feet with a surprising amount of ambient light and better visibility; three destroyers lie broken open at depths in the neighborhood of 350 feet; three U-boats partially intact at depths ranging between 230 feet and 275 feet.
Certifications required: although I breathed air on the three U-boats, I recommend mixed gas for all these German shipwrecks. Ironically, although I breathed

heliox on the *Ostfriesland*, by the time I did the *Frankfurt* the gas of choice was trimix.

Certifications: obtainable from agencies each of which is recognized only by itself. In the wreck descriptions above I have used only two generic classifications: deep air and mixed gas. However, each certifying agency has its own set of classifications with differing levels of training, most of which overlap with the classifications of competing agencies. Thus there are certifications given for nitrox, technical nitrox, and technical air, for example, which are concepts designed to keep people coming back for more "badges" (and paying handsomely for them). Training and experience are far more important than certifications.

Right: A contemporary German commemorative stamp.

Below: A contemporary German picture postcard.

Ultimate Wreck Diver

In May 1994 - as I was preparing to depart on an expedition to dive on the Lusitania, *off the southern coast of Ireland - Jeffrey Silverstein visited me at my home in Philadelphia in order to conduct an interview for* Sub Aqua Journal. *By the time the article appeared in print (in the July/August issue), the successful mixed-gas dives to 300 feet were already an important part of wreck-diving history. My first article about the* Lusitania *appeared two issues later. (See* Shipwreck Heresies *for a reprint of that article.)*

Silverstein titled the interview "Gary Gentile - Ultimate Wreck Diver." I had no input with regard to the title. After browsing through my library, and listening to off-the-record comments, Silverstein prefaced the interview with the following summation:

"President Teddy Roosevelt, Antarctic pioneer Ernest Shackleton, iconoclastic novelist/philosopher Ayn Rand - these are among the powerful heroes who inform the passion of the 'wreck diver's wreck diver' - author Gary Gentile. We spent an extraordinary few hours in the midst of his fascinating library of adventure books, historical volumes, and literature. Literally on his way across the Atlantic to penetrate the secrets of the Lusitania, *Gary showed us his own secrets - a very rare look into his complexity, vulnerability, and lifetime mission."*

Despite the use of the plural personal pronoun, Silverstein had no one with him when he interviewed me. We talked for several hours. Silverstein recorded the interview in its entirety. What follows are those parts of the transcript that were published.

I have maintained the formatting, spelling, and grammatical constructions as they appeared in print.

The first time you dove was there any sense of knowing that diving was for you? Actually, no. I felt fairly uncomfortable because I never had any desire to dive. It wasn't that I grew up watching *Sea Hunt*; I never did. I learned to dive because I was doing a lot of cave exploring and I found some caves that were washed out; where I had to paddle down an underground river to the point where the ceiling dropped down to the water level. Diving was just a means to an end.

How old were you? About 24. But I enjoyed the personal challenge of being in a place that man couldn't distort. That intrigued me. My first year of diving, I got introduced to a club that was diving some of the wrecks off the New Jersey Coast. I found shipwrecks very fascinating and never got back to explore that cave which was the original rationale for my going diving.

What did you like about diving once you started to enjoy it? First of all, it was a personal challenge. Secondly, it was an adventure. In my dreams as a child, I'd always been an adventurer; I lived in the city. I had parents who didn't go anywhere so I never did anything; I always dreamed about doing it. It gave me the opportunity to seek out adventure in a new realm and since I was diving wrecks, there were things to find. As a kid, I always enjoyed finding things. Diving satisfied that as well. Those three facets really hooked me — it gave me everything my personality needed.

Do you remember your first wreck and how you felt? The *Persephone*. It's a tanker that was torpedoed by the Germans in 55 feet of water, completely blown apart. It looks more like an underwater junkyard than a shipwreck. There was a place where it was not intact but part of the wreck had fallen over so that there was an overhang. There was like a tunnel effect where it was, maybe 15 or 20 feet wide and about 20 feet long and it was clear; I could see from one side to the other but I put myself in that position and it was really uncomfortable. I went through this tunnel and for those few seconds I had no direct ascent to the surface available. I was inside and it was spooky.

Isn't that penetration diving? Technically it would be. But it was like penetrating something that was so open. It was only 20 feet away and visibility was 30 or 40. It was an open penetration but it really attracted me. There was a feeling of fear, not that I was attracted by the fear, but I was attracted by overcoming that fear. I figured if I could overcome that fear, then I could get to places that other people who didn't overcome that fear could never reach.

After you tasted the fear did you know this was something you wanted to do a lot more of? Yes, and part of that comes from my military background. I was in Vietnam and I found that I really enjoyed the physical challenge of what I had to go through. . . long marches, heavy packs. When I was in school, I was pretty much your 59 pound weakling. I started a little bit younger than the other kids; I matured slowly so I was always being bullied by the other kids. Then I found that I could do the things that the other kids, who were always a little bit older or a little bit stronger than I was, that I could do those things too. In that sense, I was overcoming a childhood insecurity.

Is there anything about wartime experience that is like diving for you? At the time, yes. There was a very strong feeling of danger and that was a little bit beyond the challenge. What also attracted me was some of the sense of risk. . . where I was able to pit myself against nature. I'd been in some very frightful positions, and I didn't like them, but after they were over, after for example, the firefight ended and I had survived, I found the feeling of survival exhilarating. That became a lure, almost like a drug. That feeling, that first flush of survival, overcoming all odds. I did not like war; I did not like being shot at; I did not like the feelings of war. But after it was all over, the part that I remember was not the fear, it was the exhilaration of life.

That is an experience that many people returning from war have described. It's euphoria, and people who have not gone through battle can't understand the excitement. When I say that, it's in great fear of being misinterpreted. People think that means that I am saying I enjoyed the battle; I certainly did not.

Do you still find that in diving today? I've mellowed on all of that. I don't feel the intensity any more that I used to. At that age, I was still very close to that [war] experience. Now, I can relax a bit. I think I've gotten over some of that feeling of loss of exhilaration. I mean, it's actually almost like an orgasm that you want to recapture, you know, it makes you go back again. But I was willing to pit myself against nature because I figured I have the intelligence to prepare myself, by getting proper training, by proper equipment; all the things that would put me in control of the situation, and I enjoyed that feeling.

What's attractive about shipwrecks? At first, I had no attraction to shipwrecks. They were meaningless to me. But I soon developed an interest in the antiques that ships would divulge. Because ships went down a long time ago, that means anything you take off that ship is an antique. It was certainly more satisfying than buying it in a store. It's cheaper to go to a store and buy an artifact, buy 20 pounds of lobster. It's a matter of doing something on my own and finding something that was otherwise lost, possibly forever. I've always been interested in returning those antiquities to life. The older they were, the more interesting they were to me.

There must have been some adventure hero that you fantasized yourself as and read about as a child. Absolutely. I can't say a particular character, but I was always thrilled by adventure writing. There is very little more adventurous or more imaginative than science fiction, and so I read voraciously when I was a kid. I still read voraciously. What I always sought was two types of adventure. One was the adventure of exploration, maybe being lost on a island or lost in space on another planet. That would be just as exciting because the challenges were unknown. But the other adventure was the adventure of mind, the adventure of imagination. . . that's what drove me to become a science fiction writer. Diving didn't really satisfy the imagination aspect of my creative needs. It satisfied the adventure aspect of it.

Many of the wrecks that you go on have dramatic history. When I was in school, I was not interested in history. I didn't even find it mildly interesting. After I started diving shipwrecks, I did become interested in the history of the wrecks and have in turn, become a historian. . . On each wreck fantastic events occurred. The ships were pieces of metal and lumps of wood but what occurred on them was highly dramatic. I was sometimes attracted to a wreck, not because it was fun to explore, but because of its historic content. If wrecks have any meaning, it's what we impart to them.

Why was it was important to document advanced diving techniques in your books? I don't think I consciously said to myself, "Nobody is doing this, and it's going to be lost if I don't record it." I think it evolved from the fact that I entered diving as an author. As my agent used to say, "All is grist for the mill." I came into it from the professional standpoint as an established author. I saw it as a way to get some information to the diving public which was otherwise being withheld. No one was writing about advanced wreck diving techniques and decompression diving. They were all forbidden subjects and no one wanted to publish stuff like that.

You mean the dive magazines of the time wouldn't

publish articles about it? That's correct. They didn't want to run articles about anything that was too challenging. We're talking in the mid 80's. A lot of the magazines wouldn't even accept an article on a wreck that was too deep because you would have to say that you went that deep to take the pictures. Where I lucked out in my first diving book is that I had it published by a company which had never published a diving book before, so they did not have bad attitudes about diving.

Since you first published *Advanced Wreck Diving Guide*, what was "in the closet" before is now "out of the closet." It's been phenomenal, it's been more than an evolution, it's almost been a mutation. That's how quickly things have evolved in the past five years. I am not really swept up in the technology of mixed gas diving and all the physiology and the mixes. I am interested in the wrecks that it can get me to. Mixed gas is just a means to an end.

What I am interested in is the nuts and bolts, how you rig the equipment, how you do your gas switches, the operations — only because I need to understand those things in order to reach the wrecks that I want to reach safely. If I could find those wrecks in 50 feet of water, believe me, I would be on them. I have no love for deep diving. It's just that's where the wrecks are. These are wrecks that aren't pursued. I am still swept up in some of the challenge of going to wrecks that are difficult to get to.

Now you're off to go explore the *Lusitania*; has that wreck been dived before by American divers? There was an American diver named John Light who dived it in the late 1960's and early '70's, he did quite a few dives on it. And I hear reports that there have been Navy divers on it throughout the years but they have been pretty hush-hush. [Ed. note: Gary will report on his *Lusitania* Expedition in the next issue of SUB AQUA.]

When you go on a wreck that you have never been on before, do you have a different sense of excitement? I get excited just going down the anchor line on a new wreck because I just don't know what's going to be at the bottom. It could be anything. It could just be a fantastic fish experience, a marine life experience, something swimming by. To me, I still have that thrill. I never lost that. And it's more of a thrill when it's a wreck that I've never been on before. It doesn't matter whether it's an unexplored wreck. Thousands of people could have been on it before, but if it's new to me, I still have that thrill.

What future diving developments are you interested in seeing? I think in the near-term, we're going to see more divers learning to do so-called high-tech diving. That doesn't necessarily mean diving, 300, 400 or 500 feet. It means learning the techniques, all of which can be used just as well in 100 feet of water as they can be in 300 feet of water. In the long run it's also going to make diving safer for those people who are willing to learn the high-tech diving techniques. There's always going to be a forefront of divers who are diving a little bit deeper and they're going to be the ones who will make the changes, who will help evolve the activity and gear configuration, the operational logistics. In the long run, I see rebreather technology — which all of us who are doing deep diving would like to see — not because we want to dive 500 feet on some wreck. Because we still have the operational logistics of having to do decompression. Rebreathers aren't going to affect that at all. What they are going to do is give you "forever" to get out of a dangerous situation. And I see rebreather technology being driven by deep diving but I see that it's going to work its way down the line to where other people are going to, let's say, use the rebreather to dive the USS *San Diego*, which is at 110 feet, not because they want to stay down two hours but because if they get lost, they have two hours to get out of the wreck. Most of the safety problems that people have in the water are driven by running out of air. If it can help with that, everybody has a chance for survival. Granted, you may not be comfortable. You may be decompressing in the water for two hours. I see the technology being driven by the deep divers who want it so they can dive the 300 foot wrecks without having to carry bottles.

Do you see rebreathers being available to every day divers? I do, and although the price seems outrageous now, part of that is the fact that they're still being hand-made. When you compare the cost of a rebreather, today, with the amount of equipment that a technical diver has to carry (a set of doubles with isolator valves, stage bottles, all these very expensive regulators, computers, etc.), the cost is probably equivalent.

You have spent a lot of time on and written the most about, the USS *San Diego*, the *Andrea Doria*, and the USS *Monitor*. Why? I have never seen any wreck as productive for finds as the *San Diego*. It got to the point where I never came back from a dive without finding something. I even found things like nests of bottles or jars and I just took one or two. Every once in a while, I had a dive, and towards the end of the dive, I'd say, "I didn't find anything." So I'd go back to my little storehouse that no one else knew about. I'd pick up three or four bottles or jars and I'd bring them back so I always was able to come back with something. One of the best things about the *San Diego* was the challenge of exploring brand new areas that no one had ever been in before. That's why I dived that wreck so heavily.

The *Andrea Doria* fulfilled more of my deep thrills. . . the challenge of diving deep and then penetrating that depth inside of the *Doria*. I got a different challenge out of that and recovering artifacts from places that were relatively inaccessible.

Because of your battles with the government, the

***Monitor* holds a special place for you.** The *Monitor* goes back far into satisfying childhood challenges. When I was maybe 5 years old, my cousin took some money from me. It was only a nickel. But to me a nickel was a lot. A nickel in those days could buy a lot of things like gum, soft pretzels and baseball cards, and I was really upset over the fact that he took my nickel. I tried to get my mother to get it back for me but my mother didn't want to hear all of this; it was a family, it was all together and she wasn't paying attention and I kept crying and complaining. Then, finally she said, "Well, I'll *give* you a nickel," which told me she didn't have the foggiest idea of what was going on. I didn't want *her* nickel. I wanted *my* nickel from the person who took it from me. She never understood, and that has been more the motivating force in life than anything else. I like to see wrongs corrected.

The *Monitor* was a supreme example of proving that you can fight City Hall and win. Fighting the government meant winning, although, for many years there was no hope that I was even going to win. But that didn't mean that I was going to back down from the fight. That hit such an underlying principle of mine — the principle of ethics and the morality of civilization.

How do you think achieving access to the *Monitor* makes the world a better place? I think it sets a precedent for the future and hopefully as a guideline for other people in the future to continue to protect the erosion of our personal freedoms from our government. I think that the United States is the best government in the history of the World, so I certainly have nothing against this government. But government and freedom need maintenance because governments are run by people and people are not always motivated the way governments are established. So, the government always needs to be watched. The *Monitor* itself is not meaningful in the big picture. It's an example of the government establishing something for the public and then taking it away and what I didn't like about what NOAA was doing in relation to the *Monitor* was the fact that they were abrogating our personal freedom to visit this site. All people wanted to do was to look at it. That's all I wanted to do and I am real touchy about having my personal freedom taken away from me. That I will fight to death.

So achieving the ability to dive on the *Monitor* was a big victory for you. Yes, it was an absolutely incredible personal victory, because it was like a David and Goliath battle. You have to be willing to make sacrifices. These things are expensive but let me tell you, borrowing money from the bank is nothing like American Revolutionists who lost their lives to gain their freedom, the freedom of their children from the British tyrannies. That's a small price to pay and I think that we are born with such a given of freedoms that people just take it for granted. They should look back in history two hundred years ago and recall the time when there was slavery, when there was not women's suffrage, when there was hardly any freedom unless you were in the elite.

Do you see any future challenge as great as that one? No I don't, but I've actually discussed with [Attorney] Peter Hess where we should go next. I'm looking for causes to fight. You can't do everything. I wish I could. It's incredibly satisfying.

What haven't you done that you want to be able to say you've done 20 or 30 years from now? A lot of things that I could do in the future might be anti-climactic especially in relation to the *Monitor*. There are things that I'd like to do, other wrecks that I'd like to dive that are not necessarily deep wrecks, challenging wrecks; they just may be geographically difficult to reach. I certainly would like to accomplish more in my writing. Actually, I spend more time writing than I do diving. You read my books and say, "Oh, God, this guy dives all the time" but it's not true. 75% of my time is writing. I would also like to get back into fiction again and I would like to write more non-fiction. Now that I've done this book on the *Monitor* which included quite a bit of legal writing and a lot of philosophical writing in relation to what it all means, I would like to do some so-called political writing. I wrote a couple of articles about the injustice of the government taking the *Monitor* away and I would like to write more of that stuff in the future. I think that would have more meaning. I would like to encourage other people to do the same thing, to pick up the torch that I've picked up and carried for a ways.

Andrea Doria listing. (From the author's collection.)

The Mystique of the Andrea Doria

Although I wrote the book on the Andrea Doria *- or perhaps* because *I wrote the book - I continually receive requests for articles about the Grand Dame of the Sea. I am always happy to oblige.*

In the 1980's, Mason Logie suggested that I submit a proposal to Soldier of Fortune, *a monthly periodical that emphasized action and adventure, and that was partial to combat veterans. I had never heard of the magazine, but I was willing to give it a try.*

Dale Dye, the editor, liked my idea of a piece about my penetration into the First Class Dining Room to recover china. I wrote it, furnished a dozen underwater photos, and he published the lot - and paid handsomely ($1,000 - $500 for the article, and $500 for the pictures).

I told a straightforward story without death-defying adjectives. Dye jazzed up my prose in order to conform with the editorial slant toward bravery and danger. The magazine's main readership consisted of soldiers, mercenaries, and men who were neither but who fantasized about being macho, gun-toting heroes: daydreaming characters like Walter Mitty.

The money was so good that I didn't object too strongly to the sensationalistic style - except for the fact that, because the article appeared under my byline, it made it seem as if I *had composed the overly bombastic narrative.*

After publication, I was astonished by the number of dive buddies who told me how much they liked the article. What astonished me was not their favorable comments, but the fact that I knew so many men who subscribed to a magazine that advertised mercs for hire and guns for sale.

That was my first of many writings about the Doria. *I incorporated the article into* Andrea Doria: Dive to an Era - *without Dye's militaristic embroidery.*

Here is a more recent piece.

The 1956 collision between the *Stockholm* and the *Andrea Doria* is one of the most remembered events of the twentieth century. Mention of either vessel's name conjures a variety of poignant images: of grief, of tragedy, of cowardice, of heroism, and ultimately of great misfortune. Because the *Andrea Doria* sank at a depth that is accessible only to divers of skill and experience, the wreck has come to possess a mystique that is ongoing and seemingly never-ending. A dive to the *Doria* is one to be savored, not only for its historic context, but for the challenges inherent in successful completion.

The current may be ripping or nonexistent – and may change at a moment's notice. The water may be cold, even frigid. The wreck may appear dark and foreboding, or be suffused with green ambient light. Visibility may be poor or crystal clear. The pressure at 240 feet exerts both physical and psychological effects. Nitrogen narcosis can be reduced by mixtures of helium – but the trade-off is complicated gear configurations, and extra cylinders containing decompression gases. Bottom time is strictly limited. Proper gas management is crucial. Decompression penalties are long and severe. Attention to detail – every detail – is critical with regard to safety. There are no second chances for correcting stupid blunders. There is no court of appeals to overrule mistakes in judgment.

For wreck-divers, meeting and overcoming these trenchant adversities provide a stimulating thrill to the adventure of raw exploration into unknown corridors of blackness.

The sheer immensity of the wreck can be daunting. The *Doria* reaches farther in length than two football fields. At one end, the tip of the bow rises precariously high above the solemn sandy seabed. At the other end, a diver peering up from the rudder, which lies flat against the bottom, will see a massive bronze propeller hanging fearfully overhead like a giant Damoclean sword. In between these extremities stretches a bewildering array of decks and compartments, stitched together by beckoning corridors and slowly collapsing stairwells. Because the wreck lies on its starboard side, the decks are vertical and the bulkheads are horizontal: a distinctly disorienting feature that requires some stern mental adjustment, especially as the stairwells extend laterally.

Some divers just want to "tag" the *Doria*: to add the name to their logs in order to brag about their exploit. But serious wreck-divers want to *explore* the wreck, and perhaps to recover a souvenir. To accomplish these goals one must enter hallowed halls that are shrouded forever in virtual blackness.

Many consider the *Doria* to be the ultimate penetration dive. With the exception of the *San Diego* and *Empress of Ireland*, I am inclined to agree. Where other wrecks may be as complex inside – like a labyrinth or a laboratory maze – none possess the aura or the opportunities for disorientation. As I take a retrospective look on my many ventures into the *Doria*, my first descent into the First Class Dining Room (which I made with Steve Gatto), seems simplistic by comparison to later penetrations. After studying the deck plans, we dropped down into the darkness through a hole in the hull, alighted on a bulkhead at 205 feet – and accidentally swam *away* from our intended goal!

We found ourselves in the Chapel instead of in the Dining Room. After praying for deliverance, we reversed course, passed our entry point – a rectangular glimmer of green the apparent size of a postage stamp, 40 feet above – and proceeded aft until we came upon isolated items of china that were partially buried in the debris of dangling cables, ceiling tiles, broken furniture, and peeling linoleum. We were in the "dark zone" – a point so far inside a wreck where no light penetrates. It was with evident relief that we plucked some souvenirs out of the silt, and beat a hasty retreat to relative safety outside the wreck.

After scores of dives to the same location – and farther – I now swim to the Dining Room with the same nonchalance and comfort that I feel when I grope to the bathroom in the middle of the night.

Divers are duly warned, however: the line between familiarity and overconfidence is thin.

After that discovery dive to the Dining Room, Italia line china became a carrot on a stick: one that inspired untold numbers of divers to push their limits for an opportunity to obtain a rare keepsake of a popular wreck site.

I was also lucky enough to find a cache of Third Class china – this time serendipitously. Gary Gilligan and I were looking for a way into the Third Class Dining Room when we entered a compartment in the stern from which a transverse corridor extended downward. Gary acted as my safety. I slipped down a tunnel that was only slightly wider than my shoulders. I alighted in a "dark zone" corridor at a depth of 220 feet. Maintaining neutral buoyancy, I traveled only ten feet horizontally when I passed over a doorway. As I shone my light down into the compartment, I saw the white glint of china sparkle in the high-intensity beam.

I retraced my path to what I thought was my entry point. When I looked up, I saw steps instead of the vertical transverse corridor. A chill coursed along my spine. For several seconds I did not move, while I grappled with my reason and with the impossible situation. I concluded – and prayed! – that I had not proceeded far enough. Another couple of feet brought me to the overhead corridor. I saw Gary's light at the end of the tunnel, shining downward.

I wagged my light – our prearranged signal. He descended. I backed away and waved for him to follow. I showed him the treasure trove. I dropped five feet into the compartment, landed on a pile of cups and saucers that was great enough to fill a closet – which in fact it was: a china closet, filled with spares to make up for breakage. The cups and saucers were in pristine condition, still packed in excelsior (although the wooden crates had long since crumbled). I scooped up a double handful of items and handed them to Gary. While he placed the items in his mesh bag, I went down for another load.

I saw only the first handful of china. After that, I was surrounded by a thick cloud of silt. I worked by feel until Gary tapped me on the shoulder and shone his light at his timer. It was time to go. We went, leaving hundreds of items behind for another time – and for others whom we told about the latest "hot spot."

On some of my most thrilling penetrations I went alone. I visited many areas throughout the years. Finally, I decided that I knew the wreck well enough to stitch the segments together into one continuous penetration from fore to aft. I began by dropping through a doorway in the forwardmost end of the Promenade Deck, inside the Winter Garden. I passed through a narrow slot between a bulkhead and a stairwell, and landed on the bottom at a depth of 240 feet.

I proceeded aft under the stairwell, ascended gradually through the Lounge, looked into the alcove in which the statue of Admiral Doria once stood, ascended to 200 feet, passed through a doorway, crossed over a stairwell, proceeded through the First Class Cocktail Lounge and Bar, through two more doorways and into the Cabin Class Lounge and Bar, through another doorway into the Cabin Class Ball Room, through two more doorways into the Card Room, then into a transverse corridor.

I slipped down the corridor past two doorways – and dropped out beneath the wreck into the starboard Promenade. I crawled aft through a washout that stood two feet deep. I bottomed out at 245 feet, emerged in a cavelike structure in whose "roof" arched a doorway into the Tourist Class Bar, continued aft under the bar and into the Pool Veranda, then exited through an after window from which the glass was missing.

The horizontal length of the penetration was four hundred feet – not counting ups, downs, and detours.

Some of the greatest experiences of my life have been on the *Doria*. Sadly, all the interior places mentioned above no longer exist. China that was not recovered years ago has been either smashed or broken by the collapse of the superstructure and upper decks. I feel as if part of my life has been taken away from me.

But, continued deterioration will make accessible other areas that were previously inaccessible. In the future, divers will be able to explore the lower decks, and visit places that I have never been, because the routes through the wreckage were long and circuitous and fraught with obstructions that were too scary to negotiate.

The Grand Dame of the Sea will provide thrills and adventure for generations to come. Her mystique is perpetual and obsessive.

So You Want to Dive on the Doria?

Because I have written two books on the *Andrea Doria*, and have made more than 180 dives on the wreck, divers are always asking me how to prepare for their first dive. My generic answer is that you need three things: training, experience, and equipment (in that order).

Unfortunately, too many divers believe that, because their time is short, they can buy their way to the wreck. They spend thousands of dollars on the latest gadgets and high-tech devices in the mistaken belief that expensive gear will get them out of any trouble that they stupidly get themselves into. As with most beliefs, this one is a fallacy. Knowing how to *use* the equipment is the most important survival factor when the you-know-what hits the fan.

Training occupies the number one position in the preparation for any deep dive. In the old days, deep-dive training was unavailable because the certifying agencies considered any dive deeper than 130 feet to be

Courtesy of Maurizio Eliseo.

heresy. Decompression was a dirty word whose existence the certifying agencies hardly acknowledged. This ostrich posture has finally gone by the wayside – albeit kicking and screaming – because those who wanted to dive on deep wrecks badly enough, went ahead and did it anyway. Today, the D word is no longer proscribed, and there are ways and means to obtain formalized instruction which can help to prepare a diver for the deep water and decompression.

Notice that I wrote "help" in the previous sentence. The use of that word was intentional because training is nearly worthless without experience. A diver who has earned a deep-diving certification is no more qualified to dive on the *Doria* than a student who has passed a driving course is qualified to race in the Indy 500. For example, carrying a decompression reel does not enable a diver to know how to deploy it under a variety of adverse conditions. Proficiency can be gained only by practice.

Thus, certified does not necessarily imply qualified. To become qualified to dive on a deep shipwreck requires experience beyond a couple of checkout dives in a controlled environment such as a quarry or sink hole. Qualification can be gained only by conducting a great quantity of deep decompression dives. There is no magic number that automatically earns qualification. Some divers need to work long and hard to gain the necessary proficiency; others are naturals, and facility in the water and with their equipment comes quickly.

An insightful instructor may recognize when a student is ready to "fly" on his own, or who is not cut out for deep diving and will never make the grade. But usually the moment of truth is one that is realized by the diver himself after stretching his personal envelope incrementally. The prudent diver will descend progressively deeper so that he never exceeds his comfort level. In this way, he can work up (or work down, as the case may be) to ever-deeper depths, and under a broad range of conditions, until he feels at ease in the deep underwater environment.

From basic scuba to the *Doria* may take only a couple of years for a few, five years or longer for many, and never for the vast majority.

Finally, one additional factor must be taken into account: individual ambition. One must possess a strong initiative to endure the hardships that are encountered along the way in order to achieve a difficult goal – *any* goal. In that sense, it may be stated that *Doria* divers are neither born nor trained – they are compelled. But it takes sagacity to control that driving compulsion in order to thwart the ultimate experience that we all will have only once.

If you want to know what it is like to dive on the *Doria*, and what conditions one can expect to encounter, read one of my books on the subject. You will not be disappointed.

Sister ships *Cristoforo Colombo* and *Andrea Doria*. (From the author's collection.)

Alive on the Andrea Doria

When the book review editor of the Philadelphia Inquirer *asked me to review* Alive on the Andrea Doria, *by Pierette Domenica Simpson, I told him that I would be happy to get another paycheck from the newspaper after a thirty-year hiatus. I had worked for the* Inquirer *as a maintenance electrician in the early 1970's.*

I reviewed the book honestly: I noted its flaws as well as its strengths.

With the number of books that have already been written on the loss of the *Andrea Doria*, one might wonder if there was any need for another. To her credit, Simpson did not reiterate accounts that had been told previously. Nor did she dwell on rich and famous people: the typical name-dropping device on which many authors rely. Instead, she adopted a fresh approach by focusing on Italian immigrants who sought a better life in the New World.

Simpson's insights in this regard are original. Not only was she an Italian immigrant who survived the sinking, but she belongs to a group of survivors who meet annually in New York. Thus she was able to describe her personal story of survival, while relating the stories of fellow survivors with whom she has maintained contact throughout the years.

Simpson enables the reader to appreciate what it was like to abandon a sharply listing ocean liner in the dead of night. She describes the trauma of the event. Most revelatory of all was that these immigrants carried with them all their earthly possessions. When the *Andrea Doria* sank, their luggage, life savings, and family heirlooms went irretrievably to the bottom of the sea.

These immigrants arrived in America penniless.

They possessed nothing more than the clothes they wore at the time they abandoned ship. When a millionaire loses trunks of expensive dresses that she bought on a European shopping spree, she can afford to purchase clothing. When a poor immigrant loses her only suitcase, she has no means for replacing her garments. Some immigrants trod American shores without shoes, because they lost them in the water.

Friends and families were separated during the massive rescue operation. Lifeboats carried individuals to different vessels that rushed to the scene of the catastrophe. People were not reunited until everyone was transported to New York City, a day or two after the collision with the *Stockholm.* That period of uncertainty – of not knowing who had lived or died – was one that was fraught with stress.

Their only prospect for hope lay with relatives who had immigrated earlier. Survivors had to move in with family members who were already established in America. Adults had to find jobs; children had to live with surrogates. This is the picture that Simpson paints so well.

The author presents a theory on the cause of the collision: one that places the blame entirely on the *Stockholm.* According to this theory, the watch officer of the *Stockholm* misread the range setting on the ship's radar unit, leading him to believe that the approaching *Andrea Doria* was three times farther away than she was.

The Italian bias is obvious, for the author neglects to mention that, although the *Andrea Doria* was also equipped with radar, the Italian navigators did not know how to use it. They understood so little about the radar unit's functions that they kept the plotting equipment in a drawer! At the very least, this lack of technical know-how contributed in some measure to the collision.

The Nautical Rules of the Road require approaching vessels to pass port to port. The *Stockholm* veered to starboard in order to widen the gap to the blip on her radar screen. Instead of veering to starboard, the *Andrea Doria* veered to port – directly into the path of the *Stockholm.*

The author accuses the *Stockholm* of proceeding too fast in fog-bound seas. In fact, the *Stockholm* enjoyed a clear and cloudless sky. The collision occurred immediately after the *Andrea Doria* emerged from a fog bank.

Simpson praises the *Andrea Doria* for reducing speed in fog from 24 knots to 22.8 – a reduction of only 5%. Maintaining the presumption that both vessels were enshrouded in fog, she blames the *Stockholm* for proceeding at *full* speed [18 knots], while absolving the *Andrea Doria* because she *reduced* her speed. By means of faulty logic, she presents the case that *full* speed is culpable while *reduced* speed is acceptable - notwithstanding that the *Andrea Doria* was traveling faster than the *Stockholm.*

She touched briefly on diving. Unfortunately, she chose Dave Bright as her source. He claimed to have recovered the bodies of six divers. In fact, Bright recovered *none.* Bright's other observations are either fictitious or exaggerated. This misinformation, coupled with the prejudice against the *Stockholm,* damages the book's credibility.

Perhaps the book's greatest weakness is the lack of polish in the writing style.

Despite these flaws, the book presents an aspect of the tragedy that has never before been explored.

While I dwelled at length on the book's strengths, I minimized some of the flaws. Had I been more blunt, I would have stated that the book was poorly written, perhaps very *poorly written.*

I would have loved to have dwelt more on Dave Bright's falsehoods and fabrications, but his lies, deceipts, and embellishments had little business in a book review.

Bright promoted himself as the president of the Nautical Research Group. In fact, the so-called "group" consisted of only a single individual: himself and no one else. His website gave the "group" the appearance of substance and validity, when in fact it existed only in his fertile imagination.

Among his exaggerated claims were more than 120 dives on the Andrea Doria, *when he actually made fewer than 30.*

Bright scammed a lot of people - including newspapers and wire services - into believing that he was someone he was not. Nonetheless, people read his guff and believed it. It never occurred to them to ask for a membership list. He successfully created a fictitious persona that bore no resemblance to his real self.

He committed his worst act of perfidy after the death of Andrea Doria *memorabilia collector John Corrothers. Corrothers promised to give his entire collection to close friend and fellow collector John Moyer. Bright knew about the arrangement. Within days of Corrothers' demise, and before Moyer contacted his widow, Bright showed up at the Corrothers house and impersonated Moyer. Without giving his name, he reminded her of Corrothers' promise. He left with the entire collection, including personal correspondence between Corrothers and Moyer.*

I could cite other examples of Bright's treachery and duplicity, but you get the point. He was a con artist.

After submitting my book review, the associate book review editor called to ask if I knew that Bright had only recently died on the Doria. *I told him that I knew, but that his death didn't change his character. He let my review stand the way I wrote it, but added a parenthetic remark about Bright's demise. Bright was the fourteenth diving fatality on the* Doria.

Bright died five minutes after rocketing to the surface without stopping to decompress. After pulling the hook alone, he intended to make a controlled ascent and do a drift decompression. He was either holding onto or got entangled in his wreck reel when it jammed and was pulled upward by the attached liftbag. He was breathing trimix from a rebreather. He was diving off the Serena. *The date was July 9, 2006.*

Collapse Chronology Addendum (2008)

The gradual collapse of the Andrea Doria's *hull and superstructure started accelerating in 1996. At that time I commenced to write a detailed annual log of these dramatic changes while my observations were still fresh in mind. I appended this Collapse Chronology to* Deep, Dark, and Dangerous, *which was published in 2005.*

I continued to keep a Collapse Chronology in subsequent years so that future generations will have the benefit on my observations of the wreck's deterioration.

2006

The changes this year were progressive but not dramatic. The only part of the aft superstructure that persists with a semblance of integrity is some of the Enclosed Promenade, consisting of the inset bulkheads which are the outer "wall" of the Card Room and the inside "wall" of the after stairwell.

Forward of this area, the stairwell appears to be crushed, effectively sealing off the way to the Third Class Dining Room. Collapsed superstructure has also sealed off the entrance to the Card Room (high side) and the Writing and Reading Room (low side).

The Enclosed Promenade is no longer enclosed. The plates and windows that once comprised the enclosure have either rusted away or fallen down to the inset bulkhead. One large plate fell diagonally across the entrance to the transverse corridor, covering at least 80% of the opening and making entry impossible. The wooden planks that comprise the deck inside the one-time enclosure are extant.

The outside "wall" of the stairwell is gone, as are the

stairs. The inside wall is extant and exists on the same level as the transverse corridor and the outer "wall" of the Card Room. This inside "wall" is the outer bulkhead of the men's rest room and the outer bulkhead of the Pool Veranda. The after "wall" of the Veranda used to have a series of large windows that were large enough to swim through easily. Now the wall is gone, there is no sign of the windows, and the "roof" or "ceiling" stands less than three feet from the "floor".

The shelf that once comprised the lower "wall" of the Gift Shop (and the upper "wall" of the centerline stairwell) is either crushed flat or gone. In any case, there is hardly enough room to wiggle into the Bar to reach the Gift Shop.

The curvature of the Upper Deck is still distinct, and the hull in this area appears to be largely intact.

The Boat Deck in this area is not extant, but farther forward, two davits exist at a depth of about 210 feet (they used to be at 165 feet). The inset part of the Boat Deck is not distinguishable from debris, at a depth of 220 feet. This demolished area extends forward about one hundred feet. In some places, the deck of the Boat Deck stands higher off the bottom than the outer hull: this is because the outer "wall" of the Promenade Deck is dented downward, above which the metal structure rises until it drops down precipitously to an uneven and disjointed debris field which stands ten to fifteen feet above the seabed.

The stern separation crack, which is the result of the after section rolling aft, has created a bulge in which the hull plates are angled upward (much like a frost heave). At the same time, the separation has grown wider and, in places, it might be possible to squeeze inside.

Forward of the separation crack, it is possible to go beyond what used to be the overhead of the Promenade Deck, proceed inward (toward the keel), and rise up inside A Deck. One can proceed in either direction, but it must be borne in mind that this may be the only point of entry (and exit), and that one must go down in order to effectuate an exit: something that is counterintuitive, and that may be difficult to locate in low visibility or silt-out conditions.

About one hundred feet forward of the Enclosed Promenade, and at the "lowest" deck (just above the keel), the outer bulkhead is missing for a length of at least thirty feet. One can now descend into this deck level.

Jeff Wildermuth told me that at the bottom of the hull side of the wreck, the collision crack has created a washout that measures at least ten feet deeper than the seabed. This washout appears like a giant inverted cone that goes as deep as 260 feet. Apparently, fast current washing through the interior has created this washout.

2007

I made only one dive this year, and consequently made very few observations. The anchoring point was abaft amidship but forward of the Enclosed Promenade. Lifeboat davits were in evidence about 30 feet above the seabed. The Boat Deck was an indistinguishable field of debris and disjointed beams and plates. The Promenade Deck was likewise indistinguishable, if it existed at all.

At a depth of 230 feet, it is possible to duck under hanging vertical plates and enter A Deck. This is because parts of the "floor" of the Promenade Deck (the "ceiling" of A Deck) have collapsed. One can then swim fore and aft along A Deck. Unlike the condition in 2006, when only a single entry point permitted access, now so much of the "floor" has collapsed that one can swim horizontally along from thirty to forty feet, and always be able to exit.

2008

This year we anchored about forty feet forward of the place where the bow broke away (in 2004), adjacent to the "A" in Doria. Directly beneath this point is the tip of the spare anchor. The anchor is still tightly secured in place, appearing the same as it does in topside photographs. Both kingposts are gone. I did not see them lying on the seabed, but I did not actually look for them. Instead, I dropped to the seabed where the breakwater curves aft along the starboard railing. This is just about where Tom Packer and I descended in 1985, on the bell trip.

At that time, there was fifteen feet of empty space between the railing and the seabed. We recorded a depth of 248 feet. This time, the railing was buried beneath the sand as far as I could see in either direction. I recorded a depth of 250 feet. The curve of the breakwater disappeared into the sand. Thus some of the starboard hull is buried, although I do not know how much.

Proceeding aft from this point and angling upward, I passed the spare anchor and entered the hatchway that leads to Number 1 hold. This square hatchway appeared to measure fifteen to twenty feet across. I entered for a distance of one body length. My light did not penetrate horizontally as far as the hold.

The crack is wider than it was in 2004: approximately thirty feet wide where before it measured ten to twenty feet. The crack looks like a horizontal wedge that is widest at the "top" of the wreck (the deck that is forward of and level with the Promenade Deck), and that converges to a point somewhere "below" A Deck. Whereas before only the Upper Deck and the Foyer Deck were accessible aft, while A Deck was a small opening that might possibly be squeezable, now I could fit a truck into A Deck aft.

The depth at the bottom of the crack, where one can enter the various decks aft, is 220 feet.

Forward, there appears to be a bulkhead on the opposite side of the crack. This is likely the forward side of the hatchway that leads "down" to Number 2 hold.

The bunk beds that I observed in the Upper Deck and the Foyer Deck, in 2004, have broken away and now lie at an angle. Fixtures such as sinks have also broken away, and now lie free (although they may still be attached by means of the plumbing pipes).

Looking aft, the space inside A Deck is mammoth. It is so huge that it appears as if the "floor" of A Deck is missing, so that A Deck is combined with the deck "below" it. After penetrating aft about thirty feet into A Deck, I shone my light ahead and down. I could see no obstructions ahead of me, and no bottom beneath me. I descended to 230 feet without observing any bottom. It is possible that this huge open space is the garage.

Sadly, there was another diving fatality on the Doria *in 2008. On July 30, Terry DeWolf jumped off the* John Jack *and plummeted straight to the bottom due to an unexpected loss of buoyancy. Danny Moens and Danny Huyge recovered his body from where it lay on the seabed a distance from the hull.*

So far there has been no explanation for his failure to continue breathing during his rapid descent. There is some speculation that his rebreather malfunctioned, causing him to lose consciousness, but there is no evidence to support this speculation.

This brings the number of diving fatalities to fifteen.

I was gratified that the media has finally accepted my count of the number of divers who have lost their lives on or over the Doria, *instead of Theresa Foley's wildly exaggerated count of more than fifty. See* Deep, Dark, and Dangerous *for more details in this regard.*

Forgotten Tragedy
Empress of Ireland

One of the worst tragedies in maritime history happened on May 29, 1914, when a collision occurred in the St. Lawrence Seaway, between the British liner *Empress of Ireland* and the Norwegian collier *Storstad.* The British liner sank in fourteen minutes with the loss of 1,012 human lives. Yet only local Canadians, maritime historians, and a few wreck-divers have even heard the name *Empress of Ireland*, much less possess any knowledge of her woeful loss.

The *Empress of Ireland* was owned and operated by Canadian Pacific Railway, which combined rail service with oceanic travel to transport passengers to and from the United Kingdom and across the Canadian frontier. One could book a single ticket from London to Vancouver.

On the afternoon of May 28, the liner departed from Quebec City on a standard eastbound passage. Captain Henry Kendall was in command. Calm water and unobstructed visibility portended safe steaming down the St. Lawrence River to the seaway.

Meanwhile, the *Storstad* was inbound with a cargo of coal. Captain Thomas Andersen saw nothing awry as he conned his vessel westward along the broad reaches of the seaway. Stars shone brightly in the clear black sky, like silvery luminescent dots on an overhead chalkboard.

Patches of dense fog hung over the seaway off Rimouski, which, as fate would have it, was the point of convergence of the two steamships. When the *Empress of Ireland* encountered the haze, Captain Kendall ordered a reduction in speed. Captain Andersen did likewise on the *Storstad.* Both vessels crept forward like blindfolded children playing pin-the-tail-on-the-donkey.

In accordance with the Rules of the Road, each vessel announced her presence by tooting her foghorn. Each captain heard the mournful bleat of his opposite number. It is the bane of mariners that in fog, the molecular vibration that the tympanum interprets as sound is accelerated to the point at which sound waves reach both ears almost simultaneously, making it difficult if not impossible to ascertain the direction and distance of the originating source. Even experienced mariners can be deceived.

On the highway, the most prudent course of action under such circumstances is to stop on the shoulder and wait for the fog to dissipate. But vessels have to deal with wind, current, and tide. There was no wind that night, but the current and tide were inexorable. Although Captain Kendall eventually brought his engines to full stop, moving water kept the vessel in motion, both propelling and turning her like a fallen leaf on a stream in autumn.

Captain Andersen proceeded against the current with sufficient speed to maintain steerageway. For all

A painting of the *Empress of Ireland*. (From the author's collection.)

practical purposes, he may have been completely stopped with respect to the ground or seabed.

Each captain signaled his maneuvers to the other by means of the steam whistle, the number and duration of whose blasts were coded to provide specific information: turn to port, turn to starboard, slow forward, all stop, and so on. No one will ever know for certain whose misinterpretation resulted in the crash, for each captain testified in accordance with his own perspective of events.

The *Storstad* continued to move forward slowly against the current. Captain Kendall, listening to the collier's foghorn, believed that the approaching vessel had passed safely to starboard; he ordered the engines engaged and got underway. Flowing water had turned the liner on an angle with respect to the current. When each vessel appeared to the sight of the other, the *Empress of Ireland* was crossing the bow of the *Storstad*.

Orders were shouted. Whistles blasted. Andersen signaled full speed astern. Captain Kendall tried to charge ahead of the collier, but by that time the *Storstad's* bow was too close to avoid. The liner's increased speed merely added to the combined momentum of the crash. The *Storstad's* steel stem plowed into the liner's starboard hull amidships, penetrating more than a dozen feet. The twisting moment imparted by the liner's forward motion dragged the *Storstad* along. The two vessels pirouetted like drunken dancers.

Captain Andersen then ordered his engines full speed ahead, in hopes of wedging the collier's bow in the hole in the liner's side, so as to reduce the inflow of water and give the passengers more time to abandon ship. But the *Empress of Ireland* had too much way on. The *Storstad* spun more than ninety degrees, prying apart the liner's plates like a giant can opener before she was forcefully disengaged. After the vessels separated, they drifted apart.

Captain Kendall attempted to beach the liner on the south shore, but the loss of steam left the liner stranded without power and lights. The *Empress of Ireland* swung slowly with the current. Water flooded into the gaping wound, causing a pronounced starboard list. Employing the backup battery, the wireless operator transmitted a call for help.

Hundreds of passengers were drowned in their staterooms. Most of those who managed to escape from their cabins found themselves lost in pitch-black corridors or spacious public rooms on crazily tilting decks on which they were unable to stand. Sloping stair treads were nearly impossible to climb. Panic and pandemonium reigned.

Time was of the essence. Only a few lifeboats were launched successfully. The decks were so canted that crewmembers working the davits and rope falls had difficulty in performing their tasks. All too soon the liner rolled onto her starboard side, her funnels extended horizontally like two pointing fingers. The hull settled fast. First the bow dipped beneath the surface, then the midship, and finally the stern.

It was all over in fourteen minutes.

Those passengers and crewmembers who managed to reach the upper decks either leaped over the rail before the liner took her final plunge, or were left afloat when the vessel sank from under them. Most were not wearing lifebelts.

The temperature of the water was so close to freezing as to be irrelevant.

Although the *Storstad* was taking in water through her damaged bow, Captain Andersen *backed* the collier a mile toward the flotsam that marked the liner's gravesite. The collier launched lifeboats to pluck semiconscious survivors from the frigid water. People clung desperately to anything that floated: wooden oars, deck gratings, life rings, overturned lifeboats, and the dead bodies of those who died from drowning or hypothermia.

Captain Kendall was saved by one of his own lifeboats. He immediately assumed command, and eventually packed the boat with more than fifty survivors. After transferring the passengers to the *Storstad*, he and a handful of crewmembers continued rescue operations, working alongside the *Storstad's* lifeboats to pluck people from the water before they succumbed to the numbing cold.

Rescue vessels responded to the emergency transmission. Two – the *Eureka* and the *Lady Evelyn* – saved a few hearty survivors who managed to stave off the effects of cold-water immersion and exhaustion. By the time other vessels rallied and arrived at the scene, there was little for them to do but engage in the gruesome task of recovering corpses.

When the final toll was taken, the number of people unaccounted for numbered 1,012.

It is interesting to observe that Canadian diver Philippe Beaudry recovered at least two skulls from the wreck of the *Empress of Ireland*, and flaunted them prominently on his mantelpiece. In a videotaped television interview in his home, he referred to the skulls - which could be seen over his shoulder in the background - as "little prizes," by which he meant of little value.

In Rimouski, the Musee de Mer (pictured above) displayed one of Beaudry's skulls (above right) in a lighted plastic case as the centerpiece of its *Empress of Ireland* exhibit. Elsewhere, such an exhibit might have been vehemently condemned: at the very least considered in poor taste, at worst an effrontery to common respect for the dead. Imagine the public outcry that would ensue if a skull were recovered from the *Titanic* or *Arizona*, and put on display in an American museum.

Different cultures have different values. In other parts of the world - particularly Asian countries - the dead are revered by piling their naked skulls in heaps or mounds for all to see. Eastern values find this kind of reverence abhorent, yet hold wakes for the dead in which the bodies of the deceased are exposed prior to burial, and may be touched or kissed.

Apparently, the display of body parts is acceptable in Quebec. But then, in the United States it is permissible to display Egyptian mummies and prehistoric fossil bones, and to brandish representations of a person being crucified. The difference is in the antiquity of the person or remains - one of those undefinable quirks of human nature.

Contemporary correspondents compared the *Empress of Ireland* to the *Titanic*, which sank two years previous with more than 1,500 fatalities. Then came the Great War, and both wrecks were gradually forgotten. The *Empress of Ireland* joined the ranks of lost vessels as a mere maritime statistic. The *Titanic* was rescued from oblivion by Hollywood, which in 1953 produced a movie about her loss. Due to continued promotional efforts, the *Titanic's* popularity has been growing ever since, until she has reached truly mythic proportions.

The *Empress of Ireland*, however, has remained in relative obscurity. The wreck lies at a depth of 130 at mean low water (140 feet at extreme high tide), within five miles of land and within thirteen miles of a marina and boat launch. One would think that such close proximity to access would make the wreck a diver's Mecca. Measuring 570 feet in length, and sporting a massive superstructure consisting of three long decks that were magnificently appointed, the wreck has much to offer in the way of underwater exploration.

But the site has its downsides. The water temperature rarely reaches more than two or three degrees above freezing, even in mid summer – and there is little or no thermocline: one degree at most. I have shaken so violently during decompression that I thought my body might break apart like an exploding aircraft crashing into the sea. My hands became so numb that I could not hold my light or grip the anchor line. I climbed onto the boat by hooking my elbows over the ladder rungs.

Visibility is abominably bad. The average is ten to fifteen feet, with little ambient light reaching the bottom. Exposed surfaces consist mostly of lifeless brown wood and dull steel that absorb light. On one weeklong trip, the visibility never exceeded eight feet, and was sometimes less; I never took my camera out of its storage box.

The current can be horrendous. The best time to dive is at slack tide. When the incoming tide bucks the current, a dive may be doable. But when the outgoing tide augments the current, diving is impossible. I know because I've tried – and failed.

Due to the brackish water, encrustation and marine life are minimal. The wreck lists 45° to starboard. The two uppermost decks have collapsed and sloughed off to the hard clay bottom. After circumnavigating the hull and superstructure a few times, I was ready to explore the vast and complex interior. Now, after two score dives to her hallowed hull, I can state unequivocally that the *Empress of Ireland* is without a doubt the most difficult and dangerous shipwreck that I have ever penetrated.

What makes the interior so hazardous is not the energy-sapping cold, the poor visibility, or the disorienting angle, but the massive quantities of silt that have accumulated inside. The silt is not only worse than you imagine, it is worse that you *can* imagine. In some compartments the loose-packed silt measures more than ten feet in depth. And it agitates into thick clouds of opaque grayness at the barest fin kick or the slightest exhalation: bubbles knock rust and silt off the overhead.

It was under such conditions that I made *the* most harrowing dive of my career.

By studying the deck plans, John Moyer and I detected a route that led to the first-class pantry, where china dinnerware was stored. We scouted the area, then made our plans and backup plans.

We entered a hole in the high side of the hull at a depth of 70 feet. We descended along the canted deck, angled aft diagonally, and alighted at an open doorway at a depth of 110 feet. Because of the tilt, the doorway looked like the entrance to a carnival funhouse. Inside the compartment, the mound of silt rose to within three feet of the overhead. Dangling cables and wires stretched across this pinched and narrow tunnel.

Moyer stationed himself at the top corner of the doorway. When he shone his light inside, the powerful beam penetrated no more than a dozen feet. His job was to provide a beacon for me to home in on for my return. My job was to crawl across the mud, wriggle between the cables, pass through the compartment and out the door on the opposite side, cross the other compartment, and locate the china. Should I fail to reappear within fifteen minutes, Moyer was supposed to proceed partway into the first compartment and keep his light pointing ahead along my route.

If this undertaking sounds hairy, that's because it was.

I swam into the compartment with my accessories tucked close to my body, and my light beam playing from side to side. I kept my knees bent and my fins high: an anti-silting propulsion technique whose usefulness was doubtful in view of the low height of the passageway. About ten feet into the compartment I reached the apex of the mud pile. I ducked under some hanging cables as I slithered over the mud. In the act of ducking, my chest scraped through the top layer of mud. I felt my mesh bag, gauge panel, and spare regulators catching and bumping over partially buried cables. A chill coursed along my spine.

I could not turn around in the narrow confines of the open space within the compartment; the tunnel was not wide enough. I could either proceed, or I could back out by pushing my hands against the mud. By experimenting, I ascertained that the mud had the consistency of soft porridge, and offered little firmness to push against.

I continued forward.

The overhead cables cleared my pony bottle, snagged momentarily on the hose clamp, then broke free. I held my gauge panel tighter to my chest in order to clear the cables underneath.

I squirmed in this manner for fifteen feet. Then the mud mound commenced to slope downward, giving me some figurative breathing room. I *did* breathe easier once I had successfully passed over the barrier to a more spacious area. After my fin tips cleared the mound behind me, I spun around by waving my hands through the water. I could barely make out Moyer's light through the stirred-up silt.

Although now was my best opportunity to retreat, my successful passage and my sighting of the homing beacon encouraged me to proceed with the original plan.

Every nerve in my body was fully alert. I turned around slowly, memorizing every detail of my surroundings, and envisioning how each detail would appear from the reverse direction. I maintained strict orientation with respect to my route and the canted bulkheads: my best insurance against becoming lost.

I hugged the overhead. With several feet of clearance between my body and the mud beneath me, my frog kick worked effectively to propel me without stirring the loose particulates of silt. I passed through the opposite doorway into the compartment beyond. There was now eight feet of space between the mud and the overhead. This compartment measured twenty feet in length and fifteen feet across – on an oblique angle due to the tilt of the hull and the uneven accumulation of mud. The crystal clarity was due to undisturbed silt.

My buoyancy was perfectly neutral. I kicked slowly and carefully to the opposite end of the compartment, observing everything around and below me. I halted at the opposite doorway, shone my light into the void beyond, and knew that I did not have the courage to explore any farther. I was already in the pantry that I sought, so I turned around and faced the way I had come. My exhaust bubbles created a continuous snow of silt. I could not see Moyer's light, but I knew the direction of my exit.

My heart pounded palpably. The dive was going smoothly, but the potential for disaster was enormous, and my situation could change for the worse in an instant. Methodically, while maintaining my orientation and my height above the mud, I surveyed the room. I saw the barest gleam of white protruding from the soft ooze below me: the rim of a plate, judging by the curvature.

I dropped like a feather through molasses until I my

chest hovered barely above the mud. With my left hand I opened my mesh bag and placed it gently on the mud. With my right hand I touched the curve of white, felt the hardness of a rim. I worked my fingers down into the mud. There was another rim beneath the first . . . and another . . . and another . . .

I had only one opportunity to pull plates from the mud, because the visibility would go to zero as soon as I stirred the silty soup.

I straightened my fingers and forced my extended digits down alongside a stack of plates until my arm was buried to the elbow. Then I curled my fingers, inserted them under the bottommost plate, and pulled. The suction was so strong that instead of pulling the stack of plates up, I pulled my body down. I braced myself as well as I could with my left hand splayed out against the ooze. A cloud of silt swirled around my face. I could see nothing other than the diffused glow of my light reflecting off particles of waterborne silt. Nonetheless, I continued to pull with a gentle, rocking motion.

The suction broke abruptly. I cradled the stack of plates in the crook of my arm. The leverage forced my knees into the sludge. I could not see the mesh bag – or anything for that matter. I put the stack down where I thought the bag should be, then felt for the wire rim – to ensure that I placed the plates *inside* the rim and not outside. I worked completely by feel.

I *thought* the plates were in the bag. Crouching on my knees, I made certain that I did not turn my body away from my exit route. That was of quintessential importance in any silt-out. I hoisted the bag by its lanyard, felt the weight of the plates holding it down – and didn't bother with the closure. The weight of the plates would prevent them from falling out over the wire rim. And besides, I was too scared to spend the time. I wanted out of there!

By now my heart was pounding hard. I inflated my drysuit; it required an inordinate amount of air to compensate for the weight of the plates. I rose off the mud but the mesh bag stayed down until I rose higher than the length of the lanyard and the mesh. I felt like an awkward balloon floating above its ballast. I grabbed the bag in the middle of the mesh, and kicked desperately – no frog kick now because I was surrounded by a thick cloud of silt.

After several kicks I reached slightly clearer water. I recognized my landmarks and proceeded straight ahead. I felt significantly less fearful as I passed through the doorway out of the pantry. Visibility was two feet or less. I slammed into the slope of mud. Now I had to claw my way upward, dragging the heavy mesh bag through the soft ooze.

I knew there were cables ahead of me but I could not see them. I scrambled up the muddy dune like a lizard, hefting the bag and tossing it in front of me, hefting and tossing, hefting and tossing, hefting and . . .

I felt the partially buried cables snag the bag, but somehow the overhead cables slid effortlessly over my tanks and pony bottle. The bag was stuck. In zero visibility I had to grab the bottom mesh and lift the stack of plates over unseen cables. The struggle caused an increase in my breathing rate. In fact, I was breathing fairly hard – harder than could be accounted for by my exertions. Anxiety nearly overwhelmed me.

I low-crawled across the mud like a soldier under fire. Suddenly I saw a faint glow in front of me. One second later I erupted from the swirling silt into Moyer's face. He was hovering steadfastly by the doorway, and I nearly bowled him over because I had been unable to see his light until I was practically on top of him. The silt followed me out of the doorway like dust overtaking a decelerating car on a dry dirt road. Moyer was engulfed.

The relief that washed over me was tangible. My trepidation vanished instantly. I flashed the okay sign; Moyer returned it. We were fifteen minutes into the dive, and right on schedule. Our plan called for us to spend our remaining bottom time exploring the unobstructed area outside the pantry, down to a depth of 120 feet. This we proceeded to do. Ten minutes later we exchanged light signals, and ascended along the canted deck toward the green pinpoint that was our exit hole.

Our exhaust bubbles struck the overhead and rolled along the ceiling ahead of us. A spider crab was dislodged from its perch and fell onto Moyer's neck, where it lodged temporarily against his tank valve. I gradually overtook him. As we squeezed through the opening into the dim exterior light, my mesh bag passed in front of Moyer's face. His eyes grew to the size of silver dollars, and I heard him gasp through his regulator.

So much silt had followed me out of the doorway upon my exit, that he hadn't seen the bag of plates. He assumed that I hadn't found anything. Now he was ecstatic. He had thoughts of china souvenirs to occupy his thoughts during a long and cold decompression.

After debriefing the dive, I realized that the experience was one of a kind – because I would never contemplate such a venture again. I am glad I did it; I will always have the memory. But in retrospect, with certain knowledge of the hazards I encountered to replace my previous ignorance of the unknown, I am no longer willing to accept the risk of another excursion to the pantry.

The dive accomplished its goal because of planning, skill, and experience – and perhaps a modicum of luck. But not for all the china in the world would I tempt fate a second time.

As an afterword to the last sentence, I now have a legitimate excuse for not tempting fate a second time. At the time I recovered the stack of plates, the Empress of Ireland *was technically protected by the authority of the Receiver of Wreck. In old English law, the Receiver of Wreck was empowered to protect the property rights of owners whose ships and cargoes came ashore.*

In the old days, "wreck" referred to flotsam, jetsam, and lagan (cargo buoyed for later retrieval), as well as to a vessel's hull, rigging, and appurtenances. Salvors

could legally salvage goods and cargo that either remained within the hull or that washed up on the beach, with the proviso that all "wreck" had to be turned in to the Receiver and stored in the Receiver's warehouse until the owners were notified and an equitable distribution was made.

If an owner wished to reclaim his goods, he had to pay a reasonable salvage reward. The award was based upon the actual expenses incurred by the salvor, the risks that were taken, and a profit for the salvor's efforts and services - without which the owner would have recouped nothing.

If the owner chose to relinquish ownership, the "wreck" was returned to the salvors, who could keep, sell, or auction the salvaged items in order to defray the costs of salvage and, hopefully, to turn a profit for their voluntary efforts.

If no owner came forward, the Receiver held on to the "wreck" for one year, during which time he attempted to locate the owner. In cases where no owner could be found, the "wreck" was returned to the salvors to do with as they pleased.

In addition to protecting ownership rights, the Receiver was authorized to prosecute illegal salvors - that is, those who salvaged "wreck" and did not turn it in to the Receiver. In other words, those who sought to relieve a legal owner of his goods in order to increase the profit margin. This was at a time when seaside residents looked upon shipwrecks as manna from heaven and did not respect the property rights of ship owners, and who chose to believe - because it was in their best interests to believe - that a ship owner relinquished all rights of ownership when his ship was accidentally wrecked.

The purview of the Receiver of Wreck related to current events and to the disposition of property that held a quantifiable resale value: items that could be returned to the stream of commerce. The Receiver's authority was never intended to encompass wrecks that lay abandoned on the bottom of the ocean for some seventy-five years. The Receiver of Wreck is therefore equivalent to the human appendix - an organ that once had a useful function but which has since become vestigial.

The situation in Quebec was complicated by the fact that the Provincial authorities didn't know what had become of the position of Receiver of Wreck because such services had not been invoked in modern times. The law was on the books, but it no longer held any relevance. After some bureaucratic scrambling, a patient researcher in the provincial legal department determined that the Receiver's authority had been vested in the Customs and Excise division of the Revenue Department.

This came as a shock to the local agent when he was apprised by his superior officers of his new responsibility. Denis Provencher, wearing his uniform, badge, and name tag, met us at the dock upon our return one day and told us about the complaint that Philippe Beaudry had filed. Not content with recovering skulls from the wreck, Beaudry wanted to prevent competitors - who were more skilled in wreck penetration than he was - from recovering artifacts that he couldn't reach.

In a sociable manner, Provencher explained how the job had landed on his desk. He readily admitted that he knew nothing about the Receiver's functions or authority, or how it pertained to artifacts recovered from a long-lost shipwreck. He promised to look into the matter and to pay us a visit the following afternoon, hopefully with some information that would clarify matters.

The next day Provencher appeared with a handful of documents that he had photocopied from some old books that he had found in his office. Statute citations revealed the history of the delegation of authority, the scope of his responsibilities, and the enforcement options at his command. He quoted relevant passages aloud. Then he adopted a realistic approach that would address the conduct of our activity, satisfy the law, and protect his discretionary discharge of duty.

Since the "wreck" was no longer a recognized commodity, the only justification that Provencher could find for official intervention was, in his opinion, tenuous. The Empress of Ireland *lay in international waters beyond provincial or federal jurisdiction. By an exaggerated interpretation of customs regulations, artifacts brought ashore could technically qualify as imported goods which might therefore be subject to import duty -* if *they had any value, and* if *they were intended to be sold in Canada. Provencher determined that the one-time commercial value of the goods had been diminished by their age, and that because the goods were merely passing through Canadian territory on their way to a foreign country, import duties did not apply.*

Furthermore, no warehouse facilities were available for storing our "wreck." He asked that we make a list of the items we recovered. That night we laid out the artifacts in our motel room, and he took Polaroid photos of the display. We gave him proof of identity and contact information. He gave us his business card. If we were stopped by police or customs agents at the border, we were covered and he was covered. Everything was legit. And, on the off chance that the owner of the items in question laid a claim on them, he knew where to get in touch with us and could ask that the items then be placed in his care. If we didn't hear from him within a year, then title to the items was transferred to the salvors without further process. Thus the situation was resolved to the satisfaction of all. All, that is, except Beaudry, who had no claim of any kind to the wreck except that which existed in his warped imagination.

The situation has since changed. On April 15, 1999, the Province of Quebec classified the Empress of Ireland *as an historical and archaeological monument. In this guise, the removal of artifacts is henceforth prohibited.*

Below is one of my most prized possessions from the *Empress of Ireland*: a brass penknife with the name of the vessel stamped on one side. The steel blade was rusted away when I recovered the knife. At right is the inventory receipt that Denis Provencher gave us in case we had difficulty in crossing the border into the U.S. This receipt also gave us legal title to the recovered artifacts after the passage of one year.

THIS LIST REPRESENTS ITEMS RECOVERED FROM EMPRESS OF IRELAND, TO BE PRESENTED TO THE RECEIVER OF WRECKS.

- 28 - GLASSES
- 52 - BOWLS - with BROKEN
- 29 - PLATES - with BROKEN
- 6 - SIDE DISH
- 1 - SAUCER
- 4 - CUPS
- 1 - JAR
- 2 - BROKEN TEA POTS
- 16 - LITE FIXTURES (ASSORTED)
- 2 - TOILETS
- 1 - 6"(INCH) DINNER BELL
- 8 - PIECES OF WOOD
- 1 - BROKEN SOAP DISH
- 1 - NAPKIN HOLDER
- 2 - BROKEN BOTTLES (IDRIS)
- 3 - SMALL SALT SHAKERS
- 4 - CANDLE HOLDERS (?)
- 1 - ASH TRAY (SMALL)
- 2 - TRAYS - SILVER
- 1 - LID " SILVER
- 1 - 18" x 30" BRASS FRAME
- 1 - GRATE - BRASS
- 3 - STAIN GLASS FRAMES - WINDOW

THESE ITEMS WERE RECOVERED FROM 8/11/91 - 8/17/91 AS A RESULT OF RECREATIONAL DIVING.

Canada CUSTOMS DOUANES
14 8 1991
235
Rimouski
313

Received from the Owners on August 16th 1991 [signature]

Diving on the Billy Mitchell Wrecks

In 1975, while doing research on shipwrecks at the National Archives, I learned that a fleet of German warships was scuttled in a bombing test and gunnery exercise off the coast of Virginia some three years after the Armistice. These consisted of one battleship, one cruiser, three destroyers, and three U-boats.

The importance of these wrecks should not be lost to history. When U.S. Army General Billy Mitchell set out to prove to the world at large and to the U.S. Navy in particular that heavily armed and armored surface ships could easily be sunk by aerial bombardment, he did so by dropping explosive devices on the battleship *Ostfriesland*. The anchored vessel capsized and sank even before the last bi-winged aeroplane in the group delivered the coup de grace.

Mitchell was ecstatic over the triumphant demonstration, but Naval observers scoffed, claiming that the ship was unmanned and unprotected, and that in real life circumstances an air raid could never succeed with such dramatic prevail. Naval tradition and beliefs were unshaken by verifiable truth. One spectator who took heed of the event, however, was the Honorable G. Katsuda, member of the Japanese House of Peers. He informed wiser heads in Tokyo of the foresight of Mitchell's vision.

Mitchell persisted with such verve in seeking public appeal for a separate air force that he was court-martialed and suspended from duty. The Navy continued blindly to expand its vulnerable surface fleet. Ironically, when Japanese planes bombed a sleepy Pearl Harbor just twenty years later, the very vessel from which

Katsuda made his observations was sunk in the attack. Perhaps in retrospect, July 21, 1921 was the true day of infamy.

As a historian I was fascinated by the moral of Mitchell's polemic and his odyssey through American bureaucracy. As a researcher I was ecstatic over the possibility of discovering a fleet of lost German warships off the eastern seaboard. But as a diver I was tantalized by the unattainable, because when I delved further into the files I found that all eight vessels were sunk "beyond the fifty fathom curve." This indictment also meant "beyond diving depths."

Dejectedly, I stowed the documentation at the bottom of my shipwreck file and all but forgot about the Kaiser's sunken navy – until fifteen years later, when technology permitted wreck diving to reach uncharted realms and forever altered the concept of what divers considered "deep."

Along the way I met Ken Clayton, who infused me with new enthusiasm in the quest for what I dubbed "the Billy Mitchell wrecks." As a boy he had been fascinated by photos of the *Ostfriesland* rolling over. Now, as a diver, he wondered about the possibility of seeing the wreck for himself. We discussed the recent advent of mixed gas scuba and the gear configurations employed in underwater cave exploration, and almost on the spot formed a partnership for the purpose of developing similar techniques for use in the uncontrolled environment of the open ocean.

A preliminary dive to the U.S. battleship *Washington*, sunk nearby in 290 feet, established in our minds the nonfeasibility of doing a deeper dive on air. There was also the problem of locating the *Ostfriesland*. We calculated a rough position from historical data, then compared it with loran co-ordinates obtained from commercial fishing hangs. On an unrelated charter that passed by the vicinity, Clayton had the captain run over the most likely spot. The depth recorder drew a picture of a wreck so large that it could be nothing other than the long lost German battleship. The wreck lay 380 feet deep. We decided to dive on it anyway. The year was 1990.

Since Bill Hamilton was providing cave divers with proposed helium mixes and decompression schedules, we asked him to do the same for us. We had no hand in this phase of the operation other than to give him the maximum depth of the dive. His computer program determined the proper mixes to breathe on the way down and on the bottom, and generated the stops, times, and nitrox blends for decompression.

Our original concept called for four divers to descend to the wreck in pairs, but after sifting through the few who had the experience to conduct such a dive, the only person willing to take the plunge was Pete Manchee, so we settled on a single team of three.

To establish in-water traverse lines, to transport decompression gases to the hang stations, and to handle unanticipated occurrences, we required a team of dedicated support divers. These were selected less by ability than by availability: not only did they have to volunteer their time but they had to pay for their spot on the boat as well. Thus they rendered financial support as well as life support.

In the event, our support divers accounted for themselves with exceptional zeal and competence. They got to dive on other wrecks before and after the primary objective was achieved. Their role in the successful completion of the dive was in no way subsidiary to ours, but equally as important. Hopefully, they found the experience educational and worthwhile. We couldn't have done it without their able assistance.

We had no difficulty obtaining gas. We ordered heliox from Potomac Air Gas, a commercial gas supplier which has facilities in many East Coast states. Potomac Air Gas delivered the precise blend prescribed by Hamilton's specifications. The problem then was transfilling the gas from the storage bottles to our scuba cylinders. This was done by Mike Parks, a commercial diver who also owned a recreational dive shop in Baltimore, Maryland. He was a longtime friend, and

Bombardment of the *Ostfriesland.* (Courtesy of the National Archives.)

one of the few people in the industry who had a booster pump and the esoteric knowledge to handle the job.

The final and indispensable item needed for the mission was a surface support vessel with long-range capability, overnight accommodations, and capacity for all the extra equipment and support personnel. Again we lucked out, this time finding the *Miss Lindsey* out of Virginia Beach, Virginia, whose owner and skipper, Mike Hillier, was willing to accept the responsibility of hosting an admittedly risky operation.

The major logistical complication was geography. Pete Manchee lived in South Carolina, six hundred miles from my house in Philadelphia. Ken Clayton was a resident of the Washington, DC area. Our tanks had to rendezvous in Baltimore and carpool to Virginia Beach. The support divers came from half a dozen States. And the Billy Mitchell wrecks lay sixty miles offshore, some eighty miles from the inlet. Fortunately, gasoline and diesel fuel were easily obtainable. Time and timing were watchwords in this regard.

Because so much of our design plan was new and untried, and because the implementation was so complex, we couldn't predict with precision every detail of the dive – the ocean is a fickle place. So we erred on the side of caution. What may seem cumbersome today appeared barely adequate at the time. On the way down we breathed a travel mix of heliox-16, which we carried in two side-slung tanks. At 320 feet we switched to back-mounted heliox-12, our bottom mix. During the ascent we switched back to our travel mix at 320 feet, which we continued to breathe to our first decompression stop at 180 feet and on up to 140 feet.

A support diver was assigned to each of us; mine was Ronny Bell. He met me on the anchor at 130 feet, removed a side-slung bottle of heliox-16 and replaced it with a tank of nitrox-32. Later, at 70 feet, he exchanged my other side-slung for a tank of nitrox-50. Oxygen was surface supplied from storage bottles on deck and fed down to us through long hoses with the regulators dangling at 20 feet. If Bell showed up late or not at all, my decompression would have been seriously compromised, so back-up support divers were prepared to take his place. Everyone was briefed completely on all aspects of the operation.

We each carried a line reel and a flotation device for emergency deployment in the case of going adrift. The line could establish vertical reference and the flotation device could act as a surface marker. To offset the cold at depth and during the two-hour decompression, we inflated our drysuits with argon from a pony bottle.

The trip did not go without its hitches. Initial weather conditions were less than optimal, but because we built in extra time we were able to wait it out. Clayton lost some gas from his tanks and was forced to shorten his bottom time. The grapnel slipped while we were on the wreck, curtailing exploration out of sight of the anchor line, although we managed to reset the hook.

The decompression phase of the dive went flawlessly and our objective was achieved, demonstrating, I suppose, that overemphasis on planning and paranoia about back-ups and contingencies were appropriate deep diving tactics.

There is no chance now that the *Ostfriesland* or Billy Mitchell's place in history will be forgotten. Together they provided the launching pad for a new era of deep wreck-diving – one that has barely begun.

Diving the Kaiser's U-boats

At a depth of 200 feet, the cerulean blue water below showed no sign of ending. I raised my eyebrows at my buddy, Ken Clayton. He shrugged. The current was strong and my arms were feeling the strain of the pull down the anchor line. We paused for a moment to rest. It wasn't good to get out of breath at depth, so we paced ourselves accordingly. We didn't know how deep we had to go to touch the wreck that we hoped lay silently on the bottom.

At 210 feet the water continued greenish blue and featureless. At 220 it was the same. At 230 I began to see a dim ghostly outline. At 240 the shadowy shape took on definite form. It was the hull of a sunken ship.

Ambient light visibility was nearly 50 feet, the result of Gulf Stream intrusion which sometimes brushes the offshore waters of Virginia. At 250 feet I could see the hull distinctly. The side facing us rose vertically to an upper edge that curved back to form the deck; the plating was remarkably well preserved. The thinly encrusted metal cast little reflected light, and the overall dull gray was mottled with splotches of lighter shades in a nearly monochromatic design.

What I could see of the wreck so far looked very much like a submarine.

My exhilaration turned to anxiety when I saw that the grapnel had not hooked the hull, but the sand!

The grapnel had dragged over the top of the wreck, fallen to the white sandy bottom on the down-current side, and snagged with a single tine on something that lay completely buried. With a viselike grip on the anchor line in case the grapnel suddenly came free, I dropped to the sand to examine the stability of the hook.

Although only one tine had caught, it was gripped firmly on the edge of a thick steel plate only a foot from where the hull met the sand. No matter how hard I twisted and yanked, I could not move the grapnel – and the boat up above to which it was secured – against the force of the current. I raised my eyebrows at Ken, who hovered above me and oversaw my actions. He nodded.

I let got of the line. Instinctively I felt behind my tanks for my decompression reel, just in case. My depth gauge registered 266 feet. We kicked upward and alighted upon the deck about fifteen feet above the bottom. What looked like the end extended to our left, so we went right.

In just a minute or two we reached an upthrust structure that was distinctly discernible as a conning tower. And not the conning tower of an American sub, but a German U-boat.

And not just any U-boat, but a World War *One* U-boat.

Specifically, the *U-140*.

At that moment, Ken and I became the first divers in the world to touch a sunken World War One U-boat in American waters.

Germany launched a deadly U-boat offensive

U-140. (Courtesy of the National Archives.)

against the American eastern seaboard in 1918. During a six-month spree, half a dozen U-boats spread death and destruction among neutral and allied merchant shipping, sail and steam, resulting in the loss of more than one hundred vessels, including the U.S. armored cruiser *San Diego*. These U-boats laid mines along shipping lanes and in harbor approaches, shelled unarmed merchantmen, placed bombs in the holds of captured vessels and set their crews adrift, and torpedoed ships without warning – all as part of the Kaiser's bid to dominate the world.

The *U-140* accounted for seven of these shipping losses, totaling 30,594 tons. Now the Hun lies in an unmarked grave in the same ocean where its victims lie equally unmarked.

The discovery of the *U-140* was part of a long-term deep-water project which Ken and I initiated in 1989. In that year, after six aborted attempts, we reached the site of the U.S. battleship *Washington*. Although the wreck lay 290 feet deep, we conducted the dive on air, lulled deeper than we anticipated because of the deceptive reading on the boat's depth recorder, and by visibility that can only be described as seductive.

After that dive we decided to get technical. No mixed gas training programs existed at the time – the phrase "technical diving" had not yet come into vogue – so we learned "on the job" how to take a high-tech diving operation on the road, or, more accurately, on the ocean. We followed the advice of experienced cave divers who breathed mixed gas on deep underground penetrations. We adapted their techniques where appropriate, and invented our own to meet the uncontrolled conditions of the open-ocean environment. These initiatives enabled us to dive the German battleship *Ostfriesland* on mixed gas – but that's another story. This chapter is about U-boats.

Both Ken and I curried the favor of fishing boat captains who shared with us their "hang" logs. A hang log is a list of coordinates – loran or GPS numbers – on which commercial trawling vessels have "hung" or snagged their nets. In order to avoid losing additional expensive gear, trawler captains maintain records of nasty places to shun. Most hangs are boulders, ledges, or geological outcrops. About one in ten is a shipwreck.

The next U-boat on our discovery agenda was the *UB-148.* According to our historical documentation, the wreck lay close to the *U-140* in about the same depth. We had promising numbers. On a subsequent trip, we anchored into the *U-140* for the benefit of those who hadn't dived it before. The rest of us saved our surface interval and waited to dive the "new" U-boat – hoping, of course, that we could find it.

Chris Stone went down alone. When he returned, Mike Hillier, skipper of the *Miss Lindsey,* couldn't get the grapnel out. Stone bounced down and cut the tines free from the net in which they were snagged. Afterward, listening to Stone describing the wreck, Ken and I had a creepy feeling that either he had been narced the whole time despite breathing mixed gas, or . . .

. . . Hillier had gotten the numbers mixed up and took us to the wrong coordinates. Thus Chris Stone made not only the first dive on the *UB-148*, but the first *two* dives!

With the wreck rehooked, Ken and I dived separately and alone, although our paths crossed several times on the bottom and on the anchor line: characteristic wreck-diving buddy technique. Thirty feet of ambient light graced the bottom, but I cringed when I saw how

UB-148. (Courtesy of the Submarine Force Library and Museum.)

tenuous the grapnel was set: it had caught in a twisted knot of netting that was stretched taught to a point some fifteen feet away from a break in the hull. The strain of the boat prevented me from budging the grapnel in order to reset it in metal. When I examined the net closely I saw with relief that within the mass of rope and twine a thick steel cable lay embedded. I went exploring.

About twenty feet of the bow had been blown off, exposing two long bronze torpedo tubes, one of which lay almost completely free and appeared to be easily recoverable. The ten-foot gap between the forward compartment and the pressure hull was knitted together by the net in which the grapnel was hooked. The wreck sat upright, and the shell of the conning tower rose about eight above the rusting deck. Twenty feet off the port side of the conning tower, a string of buoys floated a net off the bottom like a thick lace curtain suspended from rods. Abaft the conning tower on top of the hull gaped a hole the size of a double door. I should have been able to peer into the engine room, but the interior was filled with sand and silt to within three feet of the rim.

The depth to the bottom was 274 feet.

The damage sustained by both of these U-boats was inflicted by naval shellfire, not as a casualty of war but as part of a gunnery test.

After the cessation of hostilities, a small fleet of German warships was brought to the United States as war reparations: six U-boats, three destroyers, a cruiser, and a battleship. The U-boats became tourist attractions after all eleven warships were examined minutely by naval engineers. Then they were all scuttled in accordance with the terms of the Naval Limitation Treaty.

One U-boat was scuttled off the California coast, another in Lake Michigan, a third in deep water off the Atlantic continental shelf. None has ever been dived. The remaining U-boats and warships were put down in an area known as the Southern Drill Grounds, which is where we found them. Their disposal was not wasted.

In 1921, Brigadier General Billy Mitchell set out to prove to the world at large and to the U.S. Navy in particular that warships had lost the supremacy of the sea that they had enjoyed since man's early conflicts. Capital ships had been superseded by a recent invention: the airplane. He proposed to demonstrate the concept of airborne superiority by bombing warships from the air. The German relics served his purposes admirably.

The *U-140* and the *UB-148* were shelled by surface vessels, but the *U-117* was sunk by aerial bombardment from Billy Mitchell's planes. The reason we looked for the *U-117* last, despite its importance in our overall quest to dive those particular vessels that were sunk by Mitchell's bombers, was a function of progressive depth exploration. Naval records indicated that the *U-117* went down where the water was 300 feet deep. We were working our way down, so to speak.

From historical accounts we chose the most probable location and correlated it with the hang numbers that we had in the area. After hours of searching with no result, we resignedly moved off site to check out another set of numbers nearby, but only 230 feet deep. Any unexplored wreck could be interesting.

This time we got lucky and found the numbers right on target. Ken Clayton and Peter Hess went down first. Just as they began their ascent the grapnel pulled out and the boat went adrift, so the rest of us had to wait out their decompression before entertaining the possibility of a dive. When they finally surfaced, we were as astonished as they to learn that the wreck was that of a submarine!

I knew of three U.S. submarines that had been scuttled off the Virginia coast, and concluded that we must have stumbled onto one of them. When we rehooked, the anchor chain fell across the edge of the conning tower, which I studied in detail without observing anything that provided clues to the sub's identity. Dark, dismal conditions prevailed on the bottom, almost like a night dive. I didn't stray far.

For two years we agonized over which sub it could

be. Then we returned on a day when visibility exceeded fifty feet ambient. I took a grand tour from end to end. It was immediately obvious how the wreck's location became known: the towing yokes of two trawler rigs - expensive shipwreck locator devices - were firmly implanted in the starboard hull.

Not until I examined the stern carefully and compared my drawing with historical photos did I recognize the distinctive slope as the after deck above the minelaying tubes. It was the *U-117* all along, misplaced by both leagues and fathoms.

Through those tubes once slid the mines that sank the *Chaparra* and the *San Saba* off the New Jersey coast, the *Saetia* off Maryland, and the *Mirlo* off North Carolina. Through one of the tubes in the bow sped the torpedo that sank the *Sommerstad* off Long Island's southern shore, in that long ago August when war raged over the world.

There is more to behold and explore on these wrecks than I have seen for myself or described. They are three of a kind, if you will, together comprising a rare insight into Germany's first undersea and most effective killing machine, and the precursor of deadly events to come a generation later.

To dive on the Kaiser's U-boats is to touch the heart of history. They are waiting for you silently. Go see them.

U-117. Note the distinctive slope on the after deck above the minelaying tubes. (Courtesy of North Carolina Division of Archives and History, Raleigh.)

The Spectacular President Coolidge

The *President Coolidge* is advertised as the world's largest accessible shipwreck. The operative word here is "accessible." Other shipwrecks are larger but lie in deep water far from land. The *President Coolidge* is a shore dive.

The *President Coolidge* began her career in 1931 as a luxurious passenger liner in the service of the American President Line. Along with other vessels that were named after deceased American presidents, she transported passengers between San Francisco (her home port of call) and the tropical islands of the Pacific. The 654-foot liner cost 9 million dollars to build.

The most significant event of her peacetime career occurred on March 6, 1937, when she collided with the tanker *Frank H. Buck*, within sight of the Golden Gate Bridge. The tanker sank. The *President Coolidge* suffered a severely damaged stem.

After the onset of World War Two, the liner was requisitioned by the War Department and was converted for use as a troop ship. Gone was much of the splendor of her civilian days. The addition of bunk beds and hammocks permitted the former liner to accommodate as many as 5,000 soldiers who were on their way to battle the Japanese. The liner's spacious cargo holds enabled her to carry much-needed supplies and materiel to the fighting front. For protection against enemy attack, the liner was fitted with deck guns and anti-aircraft guns.

The *President Coolidge* departed Noumea, New Caledonia on October 24, 1942. On board were 290 officers and crewmembers, approximately 4,800 sol-

Hard aground. (Courtesy of the National Archives.)

diers, and a 3 million dollar cargo consisting largely of trucks, tractors, tires, ambulances, generators, air compressors, munitions, artillery, and quinine. Two days later found the liner approaching Espiritu Santo, the largest island in the New Hebrides archipelago. Captain Henry Nelson, the civilian master of the *President Coolidge*, saw nothing in the routing instructions to cause him concern.

Then came the sighting of a Japanese submarine, or I-boat. When word of this potential hazard was transmitted to vessels in the vicinity, the *President Coolidge* was directed to anchor off Luganville, on Espiritu Santo, for the night.

On patrol in the area was the American destroyer *Sterett*. The *Sterett* challenged the *President Coolidge*. Nelson properly identified his vessel, and was permitted to proceed. The liner entered the Segond Channel. A patrol craft, which had two pilots on board, signaled frantically, "Stop, you are standing into mines." Captain Nelson immediately ordered the engines reversed. Moments later, before headway was reduced, the *President Coolidge* struck a friendly mine. The force of the blast disabled the main generators. The loss of electricity prevented further communication between the wheelhouse and the engine room.

Nelson ordered a hard turn to starboard, toward the

tree-lined bank of the narrow channel. He also ordered the watertight doors to be closed. About thirty seconds later, the liner struck a second mine.

The remaining forward momentum drove the bow of the liner onto the coral shoal off the beach. The anchor was dropped in the hope of preventing the liner from slipping off the shoal into deeper water. Slowly, agonizingly, the *President Coolidge* commenced to list to port.

Then Captain Nelson gave the order that every master prays that he will never have to give: "Abandon ship!"

It is difficult to imagine more than 5,000 persons abandoning a sinking ocean liner. Fortunately for posterity, a number of Army photographers captured the most dramatic moments on film. Lifeboats were lowered with their full complement of occupants. Hundreds of other men, wearing kapok vests, scrambled down Jacob's ladders or shinnied down ropes to the water's edge. Lifeboats shuttled survivors to the nearby shore, then returned to the liner for another load. Total disembarkation was accomplished in about an hour "in a seamanlike manner."

Two men lost their lives, one man broke his ankle, and one man suffered rope burns. Yet amazingly, more than 5,000 crewmembers and soldiers waded safely ashore over the shallow coral seabed to the white sandy beach that fringed of dense green jungle.

Two photographers capture the final moments on film: the one who took this picture, and the one in the picture with a camera in front of his face. (Courtesy of the National Archives.)

The liner kept listing until she lay nearly on her beam end. Then she slipped off the steeply sloped bottom and disappeared beneath the surface: a tragic victim of friendly fire. Total elapsed time between the first mine explosion and ultimate submergence was one hour eighteen minutes. Only a froth of bubbles marked the gravesite of a 33,035-ton vessel.

Espiritu Santo was largely uninhabited. The few natives who lived on the island were unclothed primitives who sheltered in thatched huts and who lived off the land. Luganville, the only mote of civilization, was hardly more than a way station of ramshackle structures housing several hundred Europeans. (The New Hebrides was under British and French dominion.) American forces were gradually carving dirt roads, sites for Quonset huts, and a landing strip out of the impenetrable jungle in order to create a forward staging base from which to attack Japanese-held islands. Now, more than 5,000 men were stranded on this less than idyllic isle. Many were forced to camp for months before they could obtain transportation to the battlefields.

On November 12, a Navy Court of Inquiry was convened aboard the USS *Whitney*. Such a proceeding was unusual in that the *President Coolidge* was not a Navy vessel under Navy authority, but a civilian vessel under charter to the War Department as an Army troop transport. No Navy personnel were aboard the *President Coolidge* at the time of her loss. Nonetheless, the Navy found Captain Nelson guilty of "gross negligence and culpable inefficiency."

This finding was given on the presumption that, shortly prior to the liner's departure from Noumea, a Navy lieutenant issued routing instructions to Captain Nelson. Attached to these instructions was an Enclosure which supposedly contained Special Information about the protective minefield, and which instructed Captain Nelson to take his vessel through an alternate channel. Nelson disclaimed any knowledge of the minefield. The routing instructions in his possession ended with an instruction that read, "Thence to Button

[Luganville], noting attached instructions for entering Segond Channel." But, according to Nelson, no such instructions were attached.

The Opinion rendered by the Court of Inquiry had all the earmarks of a military whitewash. Nelson's attorney contended that the catastrophe was "caused by the system that sent the *President Coolidge* into this area without notifying the Master that there were mines there." Later, a Military Commission agreed with the attorney's argument, and exonerated Captain Nelson.

These opposing verdicts neatly absolved everyone of blame. Universal acquittal enabled Captain Nelson to retain his master's certificate, and made it possible for the Navy to conceal a flaw in its command system. The loss of the *President Coolidge* was therefore an accidental event: one without a guilty human agency. Such a dichotomous ruling was a military expedience that relieved the strain of embarrassing shortcomings in the Naval chain of command, at the same time that it facilitated efforts to prosecute the war instead of a scapegoat.

Yesteryear's loss is today's gain. The *President Coolidge* is now in harmony with the sea: an enormous polychromatic artificial reef whose splendor in the realm of wreck-diving is nearly matchless. The hull is home to numerous denizens of the deep, and is an underwater tourist attraction that can honestly be described as Spectacular - with emphasis on the capital S.

Of the hundreds of shipwrecks on which I have dived during my career, I place the *President Coolidge* among my top ten favorites.

Little has changed in the New Hebrides since that long ago defense against world domination. The group of eighty-three major islands is now an autonomous nation called Vanuatu. Independence was gained by common consensus rather than by rebellion. Vanuatu has its own form of government, its own monetary system, its own postage stamps, and its own cultural heritage. Its primary exports are beef and copra (dried coconut), but it is perhaps best known for the origination of bungee jumping.

According to local lore, in ancient times a woman ran away from her wife-beating husband. He pursued her through the jungle. She climbed a tall tree in order to hide and effect her escape, but he found her and climbed up the tree after her. She was forced to ascend to the very top in order to stay out of his clutches. When she could climb no higher, she tied a vine around her ankle, waited for him to try to grab her, then leaped from the top of the tree. The stupid husband leaned out too far in his vain attempt to seize her, and fell to his death. The woman was brought up short of the ground by the vine that was tied to her ankle.

The heroic woman returned to her village in triumph. Afterward, due to the abundance of wife-beaters, other village women began to practice her audacious method of escape. Tree jumping became a tradition that was passed from mother to daughter. Eventually, men began to treat their wives with greater respect, so that tree jumping was no longer considered a necessary means of divorce.

Rather than let the tradition fade from the culture, men assumed the activity as a means of testing their manhood. They complicated the procedure by building tall scaffolds of bamboo. They made the jump more daring by vector analysis: that is, by measuring the length of the vine with respect to the height of the makeshift scaffold, by incorporating a lateral component to the leap, and by diving instead of jumping. The goal now became one of gauging the variables of length and distance, and estimating a trajectory so that one's forehead barely touched the ground – without smashing one's skull! To miss the ground by more than a couple of inches was considered unmanly.

Some primitive social activities have grown more civilized. Women no longer jump out of trees in order to avert a beating from a violent husband; instead, they obtain a restraining order to keep the man at a distance. Men no longer dive off of scaffolds to prove their masculinity; instead, they parachute out of airplanes and ski down cliff faces. Let it never be said that machismo is dead!

Vanuatu's only international airport is located in Port Vila, on the island of Efate. A small propeller plane can fly as many as two dozen passengers from Port Vila to Luganville. From the air, Espiritu Santo appears much the same as it did in aerial photographs taken during World War Two. The island is still covered mostly by jungle that is rimmed by white sand and shell hash. Luganville consists of a couple of hundred buildings. "Downtown" is a half-mile stretch of restaurants, gift shops, two-story hotels and office buildings, an occasional gas station, and two dive shops.

The locals are friendly and affable. Men and women smile easily, and wave hospitably to everyone they meet. The men wear shorts and T-shirts, the women wear gaily printed dresses. Most go barefoot.

Paved roads end about two miles outside of town, as does electricity. Beyond the pavement is a primitive world in which toddlers go naked, the men wear briefs, and the women are topless. Adult females wear skirts that consist of a single vine belted around the waist, under which palm leaves are tucked fore and aft. The people live simply and happily without the curse of civilization.

The biggest tourist attraction on Espiritu Santo – and the reason that most people go there – is the *President Coolidge*. The average day might find as many as forty to fifty divers sightseeing the wreck, and doing it twice. The proximity to shore and the mainly shallow depth make the site attainable to divers of modest ability.

Each dive shop has constructed its own entry point adjacent to the wreck (and a hundred feet apart). A cement pad and wooden benches make dressing (or kitting up) easy. At high tide, one can walk a couple of dozen feet until the water becomes deep enough to float a diver wearing tanks. Lazy fin kicks then propel a diver along a manmade trail through the coral heads to the drop-off. Next, a thick hawser leads the way to the bow, which is the shallowest part of the wreck. From there it is all downhill.

The *President Coolidge* lies perpendicular to the slope. The guideline is secured to the bow at a depth of 55 feet. The stern bottoms out at 240 feet. Because the hull is so massive – it has a beam of 81 feet – single tank divers can explore more than half the length of the upper (starboard) hull. They can even duck inside for short excursions into areas that are well within the light zone. Double tank divers can go deeper and can travel farther inside, into the dark zone.

For those who are disinclined to go inside there are many sights to see: the 3-inch gun on the starboard bow, along with its ready ammunition; two hatchways; the cargo boom assembly; three tiers of windows on the front of the superstructure; skylights; and lifeboat davits. One can also drop down through the glassless openings to take a stroll along the Promenade Deck: a non-overhead environment.

At the risk of sounding arrogant, I found the *President Coolidge* to be an easy penetration in comparison to most other wrecks that I have penetrated. The reasons for this finding are manifold.

1: Visibility is exceptional. Fifty feet of ambient light is the minimum, with seventy-five to one hundred feet not uncommon. The clarity of the water inside the hull is generally better than that found outside, due to the absence of plankton. Additionally, in many places ambient light streams in through portholes, skylights, open hatchways, salvage openings, and rust holes: illuminating corridors and compartments much like emergency lights in aircraft and office buildings. Except for the deepest and longest of penetrations, in most cases I felt that I could find my way out of the wreck despite the failure of my dive light (or torch).

2: The interior is spacious. Partitions have long since collapsed, creating passages that are more like highways than crawlspaces. Ceiling heights of eight feet translate to equivalent widths. Compartment widths are now heights of twenty feet or more. Several dining and public rooms span the full width of the hull; exploring these compartments is like drifting midway through a cathedral with a vaulted ceiling. In some cases these cavernous compartments are bisected by interior bulkheads, but even so the feeling is one of openness. No claustrophobia here.

3: Sediment is moderate. Because the hull resembles a slice of Swiss cheese, water flows constantly but mildly throughout most of the wreck's interior. This imperceptible current carries away much of the sediment that is created by rusting and natural deterioration. Pockets of silt accumulate only in dead-end compartments and on horizontal bulkheads. These compartments are small and can be either avoided or quickly exited. There is so much headroom above the horizontal bulkheads that one can swim high above them without kicking up the silt. Compacted mud has accumulated in some niches, but this mud is not readily stirred.

4: Overhead scale is minimal. No matter how carefully a diver employs anti-silting techniques, such as the frog kick, exhaust bubbles normally knock accumulated rust and scale off the bulkheads overhead. In the *President Coolidge*, the build-up of rust and scale is scant because of the large number of divers who penetrate the hull. One is likely to encounter raining particulate matter only in areas that are not often visited.

The shallowest entry point is Cargo Hold #1. One can swim three deck levels "down" (laterally) and see munitions, vehicles, tires, and so on, by peering into the compartments fore and aft. Even from the bottom of the hold one can see the comforting glow of ambient light in the entranceway. One can then exit the hold and enter Cargo Hold #2. Or, one can reach Cargo Hold #2 by swimming through a connecting passageway that only briefly takes one out of the light zone. Bullets and gas masks litter the corridors.

Other entry points are salvage openings on the starboard bow, a sea door nearly halfway along the hull, and the convenient engine room cut-out. There are banks of gauges and four engine order telegraphs in the engine room control center.

The "lower" decks are accessible through the wheelhouse windows, from Cargo Hold #2, or through the slits alongside the skylights. "Beneath" these skylights are capacious tunnels that pierce the upper decks all the way to the Main Dining Hall. Ornate hexagonal brass lighting fixtures protrude sideways from the ceiling, with bulbs and glass panes intact.

Throughout the wreck one will find concentrations of chinaware and glass bottles. Some of these items came to rest where they fell when the ship rolled over. Others have been collected by previous divers from places where they were unlikely to be seen, and placed so that later divers can observe and appreciate them. I saw hundreds of cups, saucers, plates, bowls, bottles, and glasses arranged on horizontal beams and bulkheads.

The more adventurous diver can find barber's chairs, the soda fountain, the tiled swimming pool (at 200 feet), the after guns, the after cargo holds, and the rudder and propeller shafts. The possibilities for penetration are endless.

The piece de resistance is a ceramic panel depicting a lady and a horse. This unique work of art once graced the mantelpiece in the First Class Lounge. When it broke free from its mounts due to natural deterioration, local dive concessionaires replaced it in a shallow upper corridor where it would be more accessible, even to single tank divers (and their guide).

Remnants of World War Two occupation still exist on the island. Quonset huts are still in use after more than half a century beyond their intended lifespan. The landing strip is largely overgrown with tropical vegetation, and the jungle is gradually encroaching from the sides. This landing strip gave rise to a "cargo cult" that developed at the end of the war, after which military occupation was abandoned.

Natives observed that after the construction battalion built the runway, airplanes brought loads of food and supplies to support personnel who were stationed on the island. In their primitive minds, this manna from the sky was a gift of the gods that resulted from having a place to land. Natives therefore cleared the jungle and made dirt landing strips in the belief that the gods would then bring rich cargoes to them.

These beliefs have long since died out, but many natives on this and other islands in the archipelago still live prehistoric lives, without electricity. Civilization is slowly expanding. Only a few miles outside of Luganville, I saw a newly constructed house within shouting distance of a village of thatched-roof huts. The electric meter was mounted by the road atop the stubs of steel conduits. Cables in underground conduits fed the meter and the house. Alongside the house I saw a satellite dish!

Several miles along the beach from the *President Coolidge* is a spot that is known as Million Dollar Point. The generation of the name is interesting. After the war, the Seabees were left with a mountain of equipment that was used to construct roads, quarters, a hospital, and the landing strip. The cost of shipping these bulldozers, tractors, road graders, and other vehicles back to the States, where it would become nothing more than military surplus, was prohibitive. So the United States offered to sell this equipment to the local government at the rock bottom price of ten cents on the dollar.

French and British entrepreneurs demurred in the belief that if the U.S. could not take the equipment with them, they would have to leave it behind, in which case the locals would get the equipment for nothing. In this they were outsmarted. Rather than give away thousands of tons and millions of dollars worth of equipment, the Seabees built a pier from the beach, and drove all the vehicles off the end of the pier into the sea. Today this mound of tracked vehicles makes a spectacular dive site.

These meager descriptions are far too brief, and do not do justice to the thrill of adventure and the joy of discovery one will encounter on Vanuatu in general and on the *President Coolidge* in particular.

At the cost of being repetitious, the *President Coolidge* is a spectacular wreck in a primitive yet exotic location.

One of the telegraphs in the engine room.

Sebastian

Shipwreck Hang-ups

Shipwrecks are seldom discovered by accident. Generally they are found by active searching: through published sources, through archival documents, and ultimately through the water and down into the depths. I have worked with magnetometers, side-scanning sonar, and plain old-fashioned depth recorders. But the most effective way to locate undived ocean shipwrecks is to investigate "hang" numbers: coordinates that are gleaned from the skippers of commercial draggers and trawlers.

When the net of a fishing vessel gets "hung" on an obstruction, the skipper jots the location in his little black book so he can avoid the spot on future passes. The lucky ones are able to back the boat and pull the gear free from the snag. The less fortunate ones lose thousands of dollars worth of equipment. The angler's loss can be the wreck-diver's gain. Many a time I have dived on an uncharted obstruction, and found trawl doors or a net entangled in the wreckage of a long-lost liner, tanker, freighter, submarine, or German U-boat (three of the latter).

I have spent a lifetime collecting "hang" numbers. There are good numbers and bad numbers. A good number is one which produces a sensational unexplored shipwreck. A bad number is one which produces a geological obstruction, a quirk in the bottom configuration, a biological reef, or – most likely – nothing at all. The ratio of good numbers to bad numbers is about one in ten. I have spent more hours than I care to count in the fruitless search for shipwrecks, driving circles or patterns around the point at which the numbers intersected. I have also dived on more than my share of rock piles and coral heads. But one good find can make up for all the time spent on investigating bad hang numbers.

Most divers deplore searching for shipwrecks, the primary disincentive being no guarantee of success. Few people are willing to spend their money on pure speculation. Consequently, the majority of shipwreck discoveries are made by a minority of the diving population. According to Gary's Rule, "There is a hundred percent chance that if you don't search, you won't find." The corollary is, "Only those who seek, will find." This chapter is about one search endeavor which proved eminently worthwhile.

I wrote about the *Pan-Pennsylvania* in *Track of the Gray Wolf,* published in 1989. The tanker was torpedoed by the *U-550* in the penultimate year of World War Two. Twenty-five merchant seamen lost their lives. Notwithstanding a bold tactical maneuver in which the U-boat submerged and tried to evade offensive countermeasures by ducking *under* the slowly settling tanker, the *U-550* was depth-charged nearly to destruction in harsh retaliation, courtesy of three aggressive U.S. Navy destroyer escorts. One DE, the USS *Gandy*, then engaged in a running gun battle with the severely damaged U-boat. The *Gandy* got the better of the *U-550.* Thirteen German sailors managed to escape from the U-boat before it took its final plunge. One died later of his injuries, the remainder served out the war as prisoners.

Overshot tracers ignited the spreading pool of gasoline that surrounded the *Pan-Pennsylvania.* The sea and the ship erupted in flames. The tanker capsized and settled by the stern until the fantail came to rest on the bottom with the bow still protruding from the surface. She remained in that unstable condition for more than a day, a definite hazard to navigation whose position was thoroughly documented. A combination of shellfire and aerial bombs was required to complete her submergence.

Pan-Pennsylvania. (Official U.S. Coast Guard photo.)

John Chatterton organized an overnight trip to locate this victim of German aggression, and to search for her sunken victimizer. He furnished hang numbers from his own private collection. The wrecks lay south of Nantucket, an inhabited island off the coast of Massachusetts. On the way to the primary target, we stopped at an alternative set of numbers. Lo and behold, the depth recorder spiked a solid target that rose more than 40 feet from the bottom. Chatterton made a notation, then we continued toward the main objective.

Chatterton's hang numbers corresponded closely with the position of the tanker that was given in my book. The numbers were right on target. Chatterton exercised his prerogative as trip leader to make the first and formal descent. The rest followed close behind.

The *Pan-Pennsylvania* was a bust. One would have thought that a ship that exceeded five hundred feet in length would have made an awesome wreck to explore. On the contrary, the tanker lay intact and upside down in an expanse of soft mud at a depth of 250 feet. Only the keel and the bottom of the hull were exposed. The "good" part of the wreck – the superstructure – was buried, and there was no way to get inside the unbroken hull. Ten feet of murky visibility curbed the desire to travel very far from the anchor line.

Afterward we took a vote. No one was overly exuberant about diving on the *Pan-Pennsylvania* again. Instead, we opted to investigate hang numbers that might possibly be the site of the U-boat (whose ultimate position was admittedly problematical). If we did not find the U-boat, we would return to the unknown target that we had spiked on the outgoing passage.

None of the other hang numbers produced any "hits." Plan B went into effect. Again Chatterton went down first and alone. Because the *Pan-Pennsylvania* had been such a dull and uninteresting wreck, enthusiasm waned on the second unknown. Once bitten, as the saying goes. The general consensus was to wait for Chatterton's report before troubling to dive on another potential zero.

I felt otherwise. I was always excited about diving on a previously undived shipwreck, even if it proved to be nothing more than a barge or a broken down snag. I was dressed and ready to splash as soon as Chatterton signaled that the grapnel was secure. He did this by releasing a Styrofoam cup from the bottom. I gave him a twenty minute head start before going over the side.

The water was clear and tinted a somber shade of green. At 205 feet, I alighted on the forecastle of a massive steel-hulled vessel that stood upright and which appeared to be intact. The starboard anchor lay on top of the deck. The port anchor was tucked inside its hawsepipe. There were four double mooring bitts secured to the deck farther aft: two on each side. A large windlass stood on the centerline of the after edge where the forecastle ended and dropped down to the main deck ten feet lower.

I dropped over the starboard rail to the shell hash and dark granular sand that comprised the seabed. The depth was 251 feet. After an examination of the hull, I ascended to the main deck and proceeded aft. The deck was partially collapsed at a spot where two more mooring bitts were mounted. A huge winch was mounted on the centerline of the main deck. Abaft the bitts, the hull and deck were intact. I passed two wooden hatch covers that were secured to their coamings. Then I reached an area that was crisscrossed with nets which were festooned with colorful sea anemones. Under the netting I could barely make out another pair of hatch covers.

After glancing at my pressure gauge and decompression computer, I decided that it was wise to work my way back toward the anchor line. I crossed to the port side, then proceeded forward. When the ten-foot rise of the forecastle bulkhead loomed in front of me, I knew that I was only twenty feet away from the grapnel. A doorway opened into the forecastle, and much of the after bulkhead had collapsed, leaving a broad open space that was more than adequate for entry.

I fanned my light left and right before entering. Along the centerline I saw a curious assembly which I recognized at once by the clapper inside the flared bronze bowl: the ship's bell! It was mounted on a gooseneck davit that had fallen backward off the forecastle deck. After a brief examination, I determined that the bell was still secured to the davit, but that the davit was free and clear.

I glanced at my gauges. To rig the bell properly and to send it to the surface on a safety line – so as not to lose the precious artifact in case the liftbag should deflate – would require more time than I thought prudent to spend, in consideration of the amount of air that I had remaining in my tanks. I clipped a 100-pound liftbag to the gooseneck as a territorial marker. I put enough air in the liftbag to hold it upright. Then I skedaddled for the anchor line.

I snapped a picture of the bell before I attached a liftbag to its davit.

Chatterton was decompressing ahead of me, at a shallower stop. I grabbed his attention by shaking the anchor line, then pantomimed the curvature of the bell with my hands. I was horrified when I realized that my impromptu charade could have been easily misinterpreted as the three significant curves of a shapely female form. But Chatterton's present mindset was not licentious. He was a wreck-diver, and he understood immediately what I wanted to communicate.

He completed his decompression before I did. By the time I boarded the boat, everyone knew that I had found the key to the wreck's identity. Now there was a mad scramble to explore this extraordinary shipwreck. I asked Chatterton to go with me on the next dive. I did not need help in the recovery operation, but I thought that it would be a noble gesture to let him share the experience of sending the bell to the surface. We planned our steps, then executed the recovery with clockwork precision.

The name engraved in bronze was SEBASTIAN.

After a lifetime of shipwreck research, I prided myself on my encyclopedic knowledge of ships that had been lost off the eastern seaboard. So I was vexed to admit that the name did not "ring a bell."

Five minutes after my return home, however, I ascertained the general circumstances of the *Sebastian's* loss by fire from my extensive files and library. I had even made a notation about the wreck – twenty years earlier in my research career. I had not researched the *Sebastian* further because of the pro-

Sebastian. (From the author's collection.)

hibitive depth and the distance from shore. In the 1970's, it never occurred to me that 250-foot dives would someday be commonplace.

In the meantime, technique and technology had caught up with wreck-diving.

The *Sebastian* was built in Scotland in 1914. She represented the latest engineering achievement in tanker design. Her twin screws were turned by a pair of diesel engines, and propelled the hull through the water at a speed of eleven knots. On May 7, 1917, the British-owned motor vessel departed New York City for Cardiff, Wales, thence to Rouen and Havre, France. Her cargo compartments were filled with 4,058 tons of petroleum. When she reached a position ten miles south of the *Nantucket* lightship, fuel oil overflowed and came in contact with the exhaust piping of one of the main engines. The heat ignited the oil. In minutes, the engine room became a raging inferno. Captain Falconer steered into the wind so that the flames were swept aft and away from the cargo tanks. He instructed the radio operator to transmit an SOS.

The transmission was intercepted by the Norwegian steamer *Christianafyord* and the USS *Sacramento* (a Navy gunboat). Both vessels shaped a course for the scene of the catastrophe. Upon arrival, the *Sacramento* dispatched a fire and rescue party. The fire was raging out of control, so the *Sebastian's* men were transferred to the *Sacramento*. The *Christianafyord* resumed her voyage. Despite the arrival of a northeast gale, the *Sacramento* stayed in sight of the burning tanker throughout the night. Force 8 and 9 winds commenced to moderate by noon on the following day. The *Sebastian* remained afloat.

With renewed hope of saving the tanker, another fire party was dispatched to extinguish the flames, while the *Sebastian* was taken in tow. All night long the pair proceeded toward shallow water. By dawn the fire-fighting party was exhausted, and the ship had settled down considerably by the stern. Firefighters abandoned ship when the danger of sinking became imminent. So abruptly did the end arrive that one group did not have time to reach a boat. They leaped overboard as the ship submerged beneath the waves. Five of the six men were rescued; one drowned. Thus ended thirty-six hours of exertion and hard work.

A world war was waging. The *Sebastian* became a footnote in the annals of maritime history, all but forgotten – until the discovery of the wreck site more than three-quarters of a century later.

There is a moral to this story - perhaps several. I mentioned Gary's Rule at the beginning of the article, as well as the important corollary. To those who demurred on making the second discovery dive, I might add, "O ye of little faith."

But the one that I like best is, "The early bird gets the worm, but the second mouse gets the cheese."

After scraping off the sea anemones, the bell reveals its secret.

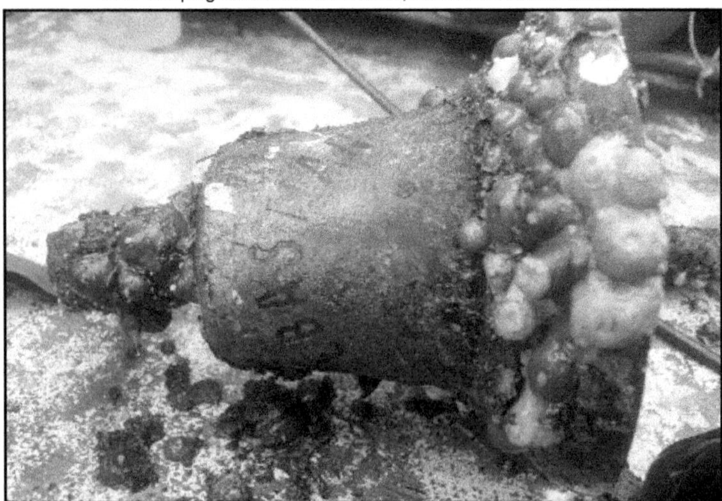

Cold War Relic

The Tower of Death and Life

Steve Nagiewitz must have found this article extremely appealing. He plagiarized it and published it in Northeast Dive News. *They say that plagiarism is the sincerest form of flattery, but I feel ripped off instead of flattered.*

The Cold War was more of a bluff than an armed engagement: one that is unknown to the present generation, and one that is largely forgotten by the generation that lived through it. With today's focus on the very real threat of Middle East terrorism, yesteryear's paranoia hardly seems genuine: a vague dream or false racial memory of nuclear devices, underground bomb shelters, radioactive fallout, and intercontinental ballistic missiles.

Even the acronyms are fading from the public consciousness: ICBM, U.S.S.R., MAD, and so on.

Yet, in the 1950's and early 1960's, political angst and anger between the U.S. and Soviet governments came dangerously close to inciting mutual assured destruction. The multitude of bombs and missiles that were armed with nuclear warheads stretched beyond the point of absurdity. Enough destructive power existed in superpower arsenals to destroy all life on the planet ten times over.

Dinosaurs move over; cockroaches take over . . .

In addition to the proliferation of nuclear armament as a deterrent against attack and foreign aggression, defensive measures were implemented. The U.S. maintained a constant state of alert by means of the DEW line: the Distant Early Warning system. The continental borders were surrounded by radar installations that could detect the approach of incoming missiles. Land stations dotted the bleak Canadian wilderness, while stations named and modeled after oilrigs or drilling platforms protected the eastern seaboard: the two sides of the country thought to be the most likely directions of attack.

Texas Tower #4 was prefabricated in Maine in two watertight sections: the triangular platform that housed the crew and electronics, and the tripod leg assembly complete with cross braces (much like a stool with rungs but no seat). The legs were actually caissons measuring 12 feet in diameter and 310 in length. In 1957, seven tugs towed both sections to a predetermined site that lay seventy miles from New York Harbor, equidistant from the shores of Long Island and New Jersey.

The two legs on which the tripod assembly floated were slowly flooded. As the legs submerged and settled to the bottom, the third leg was flooded while tugs pulled the tripod upright. Once the legs were stabilized by the weight of the water inside the caissons, cranes hoisted the platform and placed it on top of the assembly. The seabed was jetted out from under the legs so

Texas Tower #4. (Courtesy of the National Archives.)

that they settled into the dense clay to create a semi-solid foundation.

Upon completion, the Tower stood in 185 feet of water, and rose 67 feet above the surface of the sea.

Texas Tower #4 was owned by the United States Air Force, and was operated by seventy men. Personnel served tours of duty of forty-five days, followed by fifteen days on shore leave. The interior was fully air-conditioned: not for the comfort of the crew, but because the heat produced by vacuum tube technology could damage sensitive electronic components. The three radar domes (called "radomes") were covered in canvas to protect the antennas from spray. Lighters provided waterborne transportation; helicopters could land on the flight deck.

Teething troubles failed to get better. The Tower vibrated violently whenever high winds buffeted the three-story platform or rough seas battered the legs. It quickly earned the sobriquet "Old Shaky." Additional cross braces were installed above the water but there was no significant improvement. The Tower was severely stressed by Hurricane Daisy. A year later, Hurricane Donna damaged the underwater braces with sixty-foot

Texas Tower #4. (From the author's collection.)

waves. The Air Force was so apprehensive about the inherent instability that it ordered the evacuation of most of the crew. Fourteen men remained to operate essential equipment.

Engineers decided to fill the hollow legs with concrete. Tons of material and a civilian construction gang of thirteen men were transported to the Tower. Captain Gordon Phelan, commander of operations, firmly requested of his onshore superiors that the Tower be abandoned altogether, until it could be made safe. They ignored his onsite evaluation.

A fierce storm struck the East Coast on January 15, 1961. Men on board the isolated outpost registered anxiety. Snow was blowing sideways in gale force winds. At 7:25 p.m., Captain Phelan transmitted a Mayday call on the radio. The situation was so serious that he ordered emergency evacuation. Air Force command agreed to send a helicopter at daybreak.

The U.S. aircraft carrier *Wasp* was on maneuvers nearby with her task force, battling thirty-five-foot seas. She had the Tower on radar. Suddenly – from one sweep to the next – the blip disappeared. The Tower's legs had crumpled and the platform had been blown over. A few bits of flotsam were all that remained.

Twenty-seven lives were lost in an instant.

After sunrise, the U.S. destroyer *Blandy* identified a sonar target near the site of the Tower. She maintained station. The sonar operator detected a persistent tapping sound. That afternoon, a helicopter landed a team of commercial divers on the destroyer's deck. They hoped to find crewmembers trapped in an air pocket. No line was secured to the wreck. The divers descended on scuba but were unable to locate the submerged Tower.

That night the submarine rescue vessel *Sunbird* arrived on site. She hooked the Tower ruins with a grapnel. On January 17, commercial and Navy divers descended to the wreck. They tapped on the hull but failed to hear any reply. The interior was completely flooded. They later determined that shifting furniture and buckling partitions had caused the initial tapping sound, not a surviving crewmember.

Diving operations continued sporadically for the next four weeks, as permitted by the weather. A great deal of sensitive equipment had to be recovered. The *Sunbird* could not moor over the site for fear that the radomes or derrick booms might puncture her hull. Navy divers were ferried to the marker buoy in whalers.

The hoses of the hard-hat divers kept entangling in wreckage, so the divers switched to scuba. They suffered horribly from the cold. The usual protocol of decompressing in a chamber could not be employed: the *Sunbird's* diving stage could not be brought into use because of her distance from the downline. The men had to decompress in the frigid water.

After a thorough examination, divers ascertained that the wreck lay in two sections that were separated by a distance of six hundred feet. One section consisted of a mass of twisted cross braces and two bent caissons. The other section consisted of the platform and the third leg. One edge of the platform lay on the bottom. The third leg supported the opposite corner. Thus the platform lay at an angle approximating 45°. Engineers theorized that after two legs crumpled, the platform tilted and sheered off their tops, then floated momentarily as it dragged the third leg across the seabed – propelled by wind and waves – until the interior flooded enough to lose all buoyancy.

Diving operations were suspended on February 15. The Air Force abandoned the Tower to the elements. The station was never replaced. Eventually, more advanced surveillance systems made the DEW line obsolete. Saber rattling yielded to summit meetings and compromise. Wise heads reduced the size of nuclear arsenals. The superpowers became more demilitarized. The Union of Soviet Socialist Republics collapsed into its disparate component parts. The threat of communist takeover faded into history. *Texas Tower #4* lay unremembered . . .

. . . by all but wreck-divers. Among this coterie of

select underwater explorers, the Tower was a special place. It lay so far from shore that it was akin to a fantasyland that lay over the rainbow. Few dive boats possessed the range or fuel capacity to reach the area.

A trip to the Tower was a big commitment. Boats had to depart at midnight in order to reach the site by dawn. After two dives and sufficient surface interval, the boat might not return to the dock until late in the evening. Divers had to bring sleeping bags and plenty of food and drink. They had to stretch out on the deck, eat cold meals out of coolers, and pay exorbitant fees for the privilege.

Nonetheless, a Tower trip was well worth the cost and discomfort. The wreck gained in popularity throughout the years – not only for what it was, but for what it represented: a glimpse into an era of cultural psychosis and outmoded technology.

Because it rose to a depth of 65 feet, the Tower was accessible to all but the most novice diver. It was a wonder to behold.

The high side of the wreck was accessible to everyone. Stripped of their canvas covering, the skeletal framework of the geodesic radomes stood out like huge transparent gumdrops. The loading derricks that lay across the helicopter pad had the appearance of erector

set constructs. Open doorways beckoned divers to enter. Missing panes made it possible to escape from many perimeter rooms through large rectangular casements. Ambient light spilled through glassless frames so that the failure of a dive light was only an inconvenience.

For divers of experience, the Tower offered an exciting invitation to explore the vast interior rooms that did not have direct line of sight to an exit. I found the greatest challenges in dead-end rooms, down darkened stairwells, and in low-side corridors where mild narcosis imbued me with a sense of exhilaration.

On one dive I swam along a dark inner hallway where no light penetrated. I turned a corner into a doorway, and peered down a long flight of steps to the lower level. I moved forward slowly so as not to stir any silt. As I approached the bottom of the stairway I had the unnerving feeling that I was descending into a spooky belowground crypt. I proceeded cautiously, lest a monster of imagination awaited my arrival. I turned to the side on the pitch-black landing, and peered out into unbelievable brightness! Part of the outer wall of the lower level was missing, letting in light and affording heartwarming egress without having to retreat up the stairwell and along the upper hallway.

I was surrounded by air-conditioning units and racks of electronic equipment whose outer shells had rusted away to expose the components inside. I plucked a glass vacuum tube from a cluster of similar devices, and took it home. Months later, during a tour of the Franklin Institute in Philadelphia, I saw the identical vacuum tube in an exhibit of semiconductor diodes that predated solid state technology.

My greatest shock occurred when I swam into a room whose walls were lined with toilets and sinks. Suddenly a light appeared to my side. When I turned, I saw an unfamiliar diver peering at me through a glass window, where no one had any right to be. Upon closer inspection, I saw that I was looking at my own reflection in a mirror!

On another occasion I swam down to the white sandy bottom. The highly reflective granules were speckled with small starfish. When I looked up, I could see the entire platform in bright ambient light – all the way to the surface! Then I swam *under* the Tower. It was like entering a rock shelter with a tall vaulted ceiling that was triangular in shape, each side measuring 187 feet.

These are only a few of the extraordinary experiences whose vividness populates my memory.

The Tower is now undergoing a phase of accelerated collapse. The impressive geodesic domes are nearly flattened, like planets exhibiting extreme equatorial bulge. The derricks have broken free of their mounts and have slid down to the seabed. Most of the flight deck has peeled away. Interior partitions and overhead cables have fallen down. As a result of these dramatic changes, the wreck has become safer to explore. Hazardous nets no longer encapsulate the exterior, and the interior is spacious and, for the most part, well lighted.

Today, the Tower is more than a $21 million military conceit. It is an oasis in the middle of an enormous underwater desert. Like the phoenix rising from its ashes, life has arisen from the death of the Tower. Nature has utilized the structure as a substrate for marine fouling organisms such as kelp, barnacles, anemones, and hydroids. The interstices provide protection for bergalls, ling, sculpin, tautog, black sea bass, and lobsters. Flounder and goosefish lie flat on the proximate seabed. The Gulf Stream washes over the wreck periodically, bringing with it not only warm, clear water, but vast schools of cod, pollock, and other pelagic predators.

The Tower's exterior surface is daubed by nature's indelible palette – like an impressionistic painting whose original manmade contours are subservient to the scheme of color.

A dive on the Tower can be many things, depending upon the viewpoint of the individual. For the neophyte it can be a polychromatic vision. For the photographer it can provide bright-hued subject matter. For a penetration diver it can present opportunities for challenging exploration. For the amateur historian it can be a visit to the past.

The Tower is a forgotten relic of Cold War affectation. Since the sister towers have been dismantled and destroyed, *Texas Tower #4* is a one-of-a-kind museum piece whose grandeur and majesty should not be missed.

Since I wrote this article, the Tower has undergone considerable collapse. The leg that kept the platform from falling flat against the seabed is slowly punching through the decks. As the decks tear away, the platform's angle is decreasing and the highest point of relief is getting deeper. At last observation, the high point was slipping past 90 feet. Some of the majestic profile will be gone when the platform strikes the bottom on an even keel. It will no longer be a multi-level dive that novices can enjoy. But the interior will still be accessible to experienced technical divers.

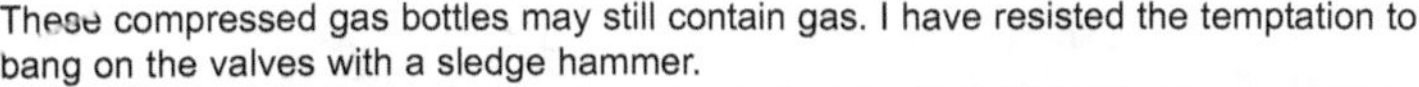
These compressed gas bottles may still contain gas. I have resisted the temptation to bang on the valves with a sledge hammer.

Explosion at Sea:

The Bow Mariner Catastrophe

Major vessel catastrophes seldom occur anymore. Strandings are avoided thanks to modern electronic positioning devices; collisions are averted thanks to sophisticated electronic detection systems; founderings are prevented by strict adherence to hull inspections and constant maintenance and repair; war is not being waged along the eastern seaboard.

The sinking of the *Bow Mariner* is a rare exception.

The *Bow Mariner* was a chemical tanker that was built in Yugoslavia in 1982 as the *Atlas Petros*. She grossed 22,587 tons, measured 570 feet in length, and had a beam of 105 feet. She was propelled by a diesel engine that generated 11,400 horsepower. She was not a supertanker, but she was large in comparison to tankers that plied the sea during World War Two, when many East Coast dive sites were created courtesy of the Nazi bid to conquer the world.

The vessel operated as the *Atlas Mariner* until July 1991, when the name was changed to *Bow Mariner*. Odfjell Tankers Asia purchased the vessel in 2000, after which she was operated by Ceres Hellenic Shipping Enterprises, in Greece.

"The *Bow Mariner* was a single side, double bottomed chemical and oil tanker capable of carrying 28 different cargoes with double valve segregation. Two longitudinal bulkheads and ten transverse bulkheads, forming nine center tanks and nine pairs of wing tanks, subdivided the cargo space. The number nine center tank was subdivided by a longitudinal bulkhead to form two tanks, which were designated as slop tanks. The center tanks had external stiffening members and the wing tanks had internal stiffening members. The tank bottoms were sloped to facilitate drainage to the sumps. All tanks were constructed of mild steel and were coated with zinc or epoxy. The total capacity of all cargo tanks was 47,000.8 cubic meters at 98 percent full. . . .

"Each cargo tank had independent cargo handling systems including hydraulic, self-priming deepwell pumps, cargo lines, vent lines, steam heating coils and instrumentation. Instrumentation included high level alarms, set at 95 percent capacity; high-high level alarms, set at 98 percent capacity; pressure sensing devices; and cargo temperature sensors at three levels in the cargo tanks. The vent system consisted of branch lines from each tank led to individual mast risers arranged in four groups."

Bow Mariner. (From the author's collection.)

Upon her most recent inspection, in August 2003, gauging of the *Bow Mariner's* hull "revealed no significant wastage," and she was found to be in compliance with all safety requirements. Deficiencies were minor: the Cargo Record Book was not up-to-date, one pump was inoperative, the crew shower was broken (forcing the crew to use buckets to bathe), one hydraulic line was leaking, and one high-high level alarm sounded before the high level alarm.

The *Bow Mariner* was equipped with two 50-person totally enclosed motor lifeboats and four life rafts: one 25-person, one 16-person, one 12-person, and one 6-person. There were five thermal protective aids in each lifeboat. She also carried 75 life jackets.

Fire fighting equipment was extraordinary: a main fire pump in the engine room, an emergency diesel fire pump inside the forecastle, hydrants equipped with hoses and nozzles distributed throughout the vessel, a fixed dry powder system, fixed carbon dioxide systems, and portable foam equipment and alcohol-resistant foam. Fire lockers contained suits, boots, lifelines, fire axes, helmets, portable lights, and eleven self-contained breathing units with plenty of spare bottles. "There were also 40 emergency escape breathing devices aboard, including one in each cabin."

Additionally, even though it was not a requirement at the time of her construction, the *Bow Mariner* was equipped with an inert gas generator: a fire suppression system that consisted of a nitrogen generator and a bottled nitrogen storage unit. Nitrogen did not actually suppress a fire; instead, it prevented fire from occurring by replacing purged gases with one that was nonflammable. "A properly inerted cargo tank cannot explode or support combustion."

In consideration of catastrophe that was yet to come, it is unfortunate that the inert gas generator was intentionally disabled with the approval of Det Norske Veritas (the Norwegian vessel classification agency that is equivalent to the American Bureau of Ships).

February 28, 2004 found the chemical tanker on a

routine passage from New York City to Houston, Texas. On board were twenty-seven officers and crewmembers. The master, chief officer, and chief engineer were Greek. The remaining officers and crewmembers were Filipino. The tanker's cargo consisted of more than three million gallons of ethanol - a volatile liquid better known as ethyl alcohol or grain alcohol.

Twenty-two tanks were empty. These tanks had previously held methyl tertiary butyl ether, a volatile and flammable liquid solvent that is used as a gasoline additive to raise the octane number. Captain Efstratios Kavouras ordered these tanks to be opened for ventilation and cleaning. Residual liquid was pumped into drums for removal. Unlike electric or spark-producing pumps, pumps that are used to move combustible liquids are sealed units called eductors, which create suction by means of a pressurized fluid that is passed through a Venturi tube.

One of the pumps failed, and was replaced by one of a different style and which was modified in the onboard machine shop because of a collapsed mid-section. This jury-rigged pump was in operation at six o'clock when a "yellow flash" was observed on the port side some seventy feet abaft the bow. Flames rose

upward and wafted aft over the pump's manifold. One minute later there was a "big explosion" in way of the manifold, "followed by another large explosion." Additional explosions occurred in rapid succession. Deck plates were torn up and hull plates were blasted outward. Fire suddenly raged out of control and quickly spread to adjacent tank compartments, detonating them one after the other like a series of gigantic firecrackers. Within moments the vessel was engulfed in flames that were beyond the ability of the crew to extinguish.

Several vessels were in the vicinity at the time and observed the flash in the gathering twilight. The bulk carrier *Dakshineshwar* was less than four miles away. She immediately transmitted the *Bow Mariner's* position. The fishing vessel *Capt. Bucky* intercepted the transmission and relayed it to the Coast Guard. Both the *Capt. Bucky* and the fishing vessel *Karen L.* retrieved their fishing gear and diverted to lend assistance.

The *Bow Mariner* listed to starboard, then slowly rolled back to an even keel and commenced to settle by the bow. The fire was raging out of control. One officer activated a distress alarm in the radio room, and "sent a Mayday call on the radio." Another activated the EPIRB (Emergency Position Indicating Radio Beacon) from the bridge top and tossed it overboard.

The stern rose upward. After donning life jackets, crewmembers leaped overboard to escape the uncontrollable fire. One landed in a floating life raft. Two others landed nearby, swam to the raft, and climbed aboard. All around them shone hand flares and the lights of life jackets. The three men cut the painter and "paddled around to pick up survivors." They pulled three more men from the water.

The *Dakshineshwar* approached as close as she dared, and lowered a lifeboat to search for survivors. Just when the lifeboat located the life raft, a Coast Guard helicopter arrived. The lifeboat backed away and continued to search for other survivors until the propeller fouled a line. The *Capt. Bucky* towed the lifeboat back to the ship.

A Coast Guard fixed-wing aircraft also arrived on the scene. This plane was equipped with infrared video, and proceeded to record the recovery efforts. By this time – about an hour and fifteen minutes after the initial explosion – only the stern of the *Bow Mariner* was "sticking out of the water. The water level was nearly at the bridge top. There were no fires and there were no people visible on the ship."

The tanker sank about fifteen minutes later.

The helicopter hovered over the raft that was occupied by survivors. "A basket was lowered to the raft twice but a survivor in the door of the canopy made no effort to climb in, despite hand signals and use of the helicopter's handheld searchlight to try to coax him into the basket." The men were numbed by the cold. The water temperature was 37°. They were suffering from their immersion.

A rescue swimmer was lowered from the helicopter to the raft. One by one he put the survivors in the basket so they could be hoisted up to the helicopter. "The survivors were taken to Norfolk Sentara Hospital, where the survivors and rescue swimmer were treated for hypothermia and exposure to oil and ethyl alcohol.

Another helicopter directed the *Karen L* by searchlight to a floating body, which she recovered.

This same helicopter then spotted a group of four more bodies, one of which showed movement and signs of life. A rescue swimmer was lowered into the water to recover the surviving victim. The victim died on the way to the hospital.

The *Capt. Bucky* discovered a lifeboat and "found a man with his arms wrapped tightly in the lifeboat's lifelines, with only his head and arms above water. The man was delirious but was making 'thank you' gestures to his rescuers. They brought him aboard" but he became unconscious. A rescue swimmer was lowered from a helicopter to Coast Guard motor lifeboat *CG-47222*, which transferred him to the fishing vessel, "where he found the victim alive, covered in oil and in great pain. The victim and rescue swimmer were hoisted to the helicopter, which took him to the Ocean City airport. During the flight the victim lost all vital signs so the crew commenced CPR." The victim was transferred to a Maryland State Police helicopter, but died on the way to the hospital.

Various Coast Guard units continued the search for survivors throughout the night and all the following day. "Active search efforts were suspended after dark on 29 February 2004."

Six Filipino crewmembers survived the catastrophe. Twenty-one officers and crewmembers perished onboard the vessel or in the water.

The sunken hull was easily located by the oil slick that marred the surface of the sea. This slick was one and a half miles wide, and extended thirty-five miles downcurrent. Within days, the NOAA vessel *Rude* was requisitioned to conduct a multi-beam survey of the wreck.

"Between 14 March 2004 and 18 March 2004 contractors hired by the responsible party conducted a survey of the sunken *Bow Mariner* using underwater remotely operated vehicles. The purpose of the survey was to search for remains, chart the position of the vessel and determine whether the vessel's cargo and fuel oil were recoverable. The survey revealed the vessel's fuel oil tanks were breached and had spilled their entire contents. The six center cargo tanks containing ethyl alcohol were not accessible, but the video revealed extensive damage to the entire cargo block."

Initial environmental concerns were found to be

This NOAA multi-beam scan shows how the tank hull plates were blown outward.

groundless, as the cargo and fuel oil had either been consumed in the blaze or dispersed by the sea. An oil recovery vessel found scant pollution to recover. The Coast Guard completed its underwater examination, but at that time had not reached any conclusion about the cause of the explosion.

The testimony of surviving witnesses proceeded quickly, yet the Coast Guard took nearly a year to complete its investigation and submit its findings. Investigators determined that the vessel "caught fire and exploded while the crew was engaged in cleaning residual Methyl Tert Butyl Ether (MTBE) from cargo tank number eight starboard. . . . The vessel's cargo of ethyl alcohol (3,188,711 gallons) was released, along with the vessel's heavy fuel oil (192,904 gallons), diesel fuel (48,266 gallons) and slops (quantity unknown). . . . The cause of this casualty was the ignition of a fuel/air mixture, either on deck or in the cargo tanks, that was within its flammable limits. The ignition source could not be precisely determined. Contributing to this casualty was the failure of the operator, Ceres Hellenic Enterprises, Ltd., and the senior officers of the *Bow Mariner*, to properly implement the company and vessel Safety, Quality and Environmental Protection Management System (SQEMS)."

According to the Coast Guard's "best guess," the "opening of all of the hatches for the empty cargo tanks, as was done on the *Bow Mariner*, fails to conform to any known customary marine practice. Because the tanks had not been washed or mechanically ventilated the concentration of vapor was very high, and certainly well above the UEL [Upper Explosive Limit] for MTBE. Opening all of the cargo tank hatches permitted vapors to escape at deck level, where the crew was actively working. This exposed them to toxic vapors and increased the likelihood of an explosion to initiate from an accidental spark. MTBE vapors are heavier than air, and there were many obstructions on deck created by the cargo systems, manifolds and midship deckhouse where pockets of vapor could accumulate, despite cross deck wind or the vessel's forward movement. It also permitted oxygen to enter the tanks, diluting the fuel-rich atmosphere and possibly bringing the mixture within the tanks into the explosive range. There is no evidence that the speed of the gas freeing process would have increased by opening the cargo hatches."

As for the source of ignition, the Coast Guard found "the possibility of an electrostatic discharge or mechanical spark from the work being performed by the pumpman cannot be dismissed."

In summation, the *Bow Mariner* catastrophe was one that could have been prevented by the implementation of proper cleaning procedures whose requirements were governed by international regulations that were not followed by the vessel's owner or operator.

Furthermore, the Coast Guard castigated Captain Kavouras for his failure "to properly organize a response to the explosions," which "contributed to the high loss of life. He abandoned ship without sending a distress signal, without attempting to contact a nearby ship, without conducting a proper muster or search for injured crewmen, and without attempting to launch primary lifesaving appliances.

"Captain Kavouras and Chief Engineer Athanasiou abandoned ship within 10 minutes of the first explosion, leaving behind other crewmembers they knew to be alive. Their premature action exposed the crewmen who entered the water with them to the cold water far earlier than necessary, and contributed to the high loss of life."

Wreck-divers commenced to visit the site soon after the Coast Guard completed its survey work. The first divers on the wreck were Steve Gatto, Jon Hulburt, Bart Malone, Greg Masi, Harold Moyers, Mark Nix, and Tom Packer. The date was April 10, 2004. For transportation they used Harold Moyers' dive boat, the *Big Mac*.

Moyers told me, "The hook landed in the very top of the mast. I tied in. In the wheelhouse on my first dive I found and took the Alpha flag from its compartment on

Jon Hulburt shooting video on the starboard bridge deck. Note how clean the surfaces appear. The doorway on the other side of him is the entrance to the wheelhouse.

the port side. I wanted the international diver down flag."

Moyers took me to the wreck on May 6, 2004 to survey the stern, and again on May 16, 2004 to survey the bow. I found the wreck sitting upright at a depth of 250 feet, in an area of clean water in which visibility commonly exceeds fifty feet. The stern structure stands more than 100 feet above the white sandy bottom, with the wheelhouse and navigating bridge rising to a depth of 160 feet.

Both the stern and the bow are amazingly intact. When I first descended to the stern structure, I saw a ship that appeared so clean and white that it might have been sitting in dry dock. No damage was in evidence. Not until I dropped over the rail in front of the wheelhouse did I see the wall of scorched and blackened metal that stretched to the torn decking sixty feet below.

When I descended to the seabed beneath the bridge wings, the true state of damage was revealed to me. The hull was ruptured outward on both the port and starboard sides, from the deck level down to the turn of the bilge some fifty feet below. Steel plates were torn and twisted like so much papier-mâché. My observation corroborated that of the Coast Guard's (which was based on fifty-seven hours of videotape), that "nearly all of the wing tanks exploded, with most of the side shell missing in the cargo block on both sides."

I found the same kind of damage in the bow. The forecastle lies at a depth of 200 feet. It shows no sign of damage, but when I dropped down to the main deck to look at the tank compartments, I saw a gap in the starboard hull that stretched ten feet across and that extended twenty feet down. The internal framing was clearly exposed.

The forefoot of the *Bow Mariner* is interesting. Many modern vessels possess a bulbous bow which cleaves through the water with far greater efficiency and economy of fuel than the straight-stemmed vessels of yesteryear. Instead of one bulbous forefoot, the *Bow Mariner* has two, giving the appearance of a pair of rounded breasts. I suppose that on a vessel that is more than one hundred feet abeam, this double forefoot arrangement is more effectual than a single.

Also of interest are the bow thrusters that are positioned on either side. The tube in which each thruster propeller is encased measures five feet in diameter, and can be found several feet above the seabed. A grate that is flush with the hull prevents entry. About six feet inside the grate is a four-bladed propeller, each blade of which is some two feet in length.

The name board consists of individual steel letters that are welded to the hull. The letters are painted black to contrast with the orange color of the hull.

Immediately abaft the forecastle, the starboard hull is demolished from the main deck down about twenty feet - probably the result of an internal explosion. The internal framing is clearly exposed.

On the May 16, 2004 trip, a group effort resulted in the recovery of the ship's bell from its davit on the forecastle. The divers onboard the *Big Mac* that day were Steve Gatto, Jon Hulburt, Bart Malone, Harold Moyers,

Tom Packer, Joe Zeissweiss, and this author.

Most divers have concentrated their explorations at the stern, where the multi-level structure affords numerous places of entry and a maze of compartments and passageways to explore.

It is interesting to see and photograph the wreck as it slowly becomes encrusted. Already it has become a marine habitat: an oasis in the middle of a vast ocean desert. I returned to the site to take comparative photographs on August 22, 2005. This time I was aboard the *O.C. Diver*, Captain Ted Green. After a year and a half on the bottom, marine encrustation and fouling organisms had a strong foothold on the exterior surfaces as well as inside the wheelhouse.

The wreck lies with the bow pointed northwest, the stern southeast.

The GPS coordinates are 37-53.351 / 74-15.372. To get directly on the wheelhouse, go to 37-53.355 / 74-15.379 (loran 26785.2 / 42083.0). This location is approximately 45 miles east of the Virginia coast.

The surfaces are getting encrusted after a year and a half under water. This is a picture of the inside of the wheelhouse. The windows face forward. For a picture of the bell on its davit prior to removal, see the upper right photo on the front cover.

Halifax Wreck Diving

Halifax has been a major shipping port since the sixteen hundreds, serving Canada ever since France first settled the North American continent. The long funnel shape of the harbor entrance creates a perfect refuge for ships because it is protected from the sea on all sides except for the narrow opening to the southeast. Add a couple of ancient forts and gun emplacements along the coast, and the town became an impregnable naval base whose approaches have never been breached by an enemy vessel of any kind. Nor does the rocky shore have sandy beaches for amphibious assault or invasion by foreign forces.

On the down side, for friendly warships and the multitude of merchantmen, are the craggy granite reefs which protrude above the foam-flecked waves at irregular intervals, or worse, which rise to within several feet of the surface and which are largely indiscernible on calm days or when fog lies heavily upon the sea, turning the harbor approaches into an obstacle course which has barred the way for many an unsuspecting mariner. And many of those, which have blundered safely through the ring of islands, have come to grief on the bluffs which rise steeply from the water's edge.

Thus Halifax Harbor has become a port of lost ships, an underwater graveyard where lie the worm-eaten timbers and rusted steel plates of vessels of all descriptions and ages. Boats or inflatables are necessary to reach the offshore sites, but many wrecks are accessible from land. However, a note to those who are not in the best of physical condition: some of these latter sites require long walks over uneven terrain, requiring several trips to transport dive gear from a vehicle to the entry point, and back again.

No matter where you dive, even if not on the site of a shipwreck, you are bound to have an experience that you will never forget, for the bottom is richly endowed with colorful cold-water marine life which will satisfy both your palate and your palette, depending upon your tastes or photographic point of view. Schools of cod swim lazily through the water, starfish creep slowly over barnacle-encrusted rocks, kelp fronds waltz delicately in the surge, and sea urchins dot the landscape like spiked gumdrops.

One of the most accessible and popular shore dives is the wreck of the *La Tribune*. The forty-four-gun frigate came to grief during a November storm in 1797 with great loss of life. Today it lies in 50 feet of water about a hundred feet from shore. Nothing remains of the wooden hull, but the ballast pile, heaps of cannon balls, and occasional hand grenades, are the centerpiece of a vast debris field, while in deeper water two iron cannons rest on the boulder-strewn bottom.

Also popular is the *Atlantic*, a passenger vessel which crashed into Mars Rock during a cloudy April night in 1873. More than 500 hundred people drowned

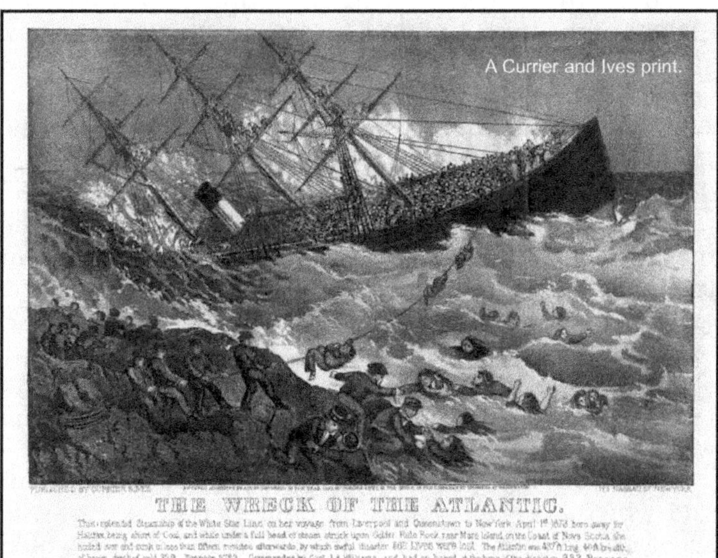

A Currier and Ives print.

The rocky coast presents challenges for shore divers. Eric Garay humps his doubles along typical unsound footing to the entry point. Dive gear is carried on a second trip.

within reach of shore. Today, an engraved marble headstone memorializes the mass grave. The wreck site is marked by the boilers and the remains of the engine, lying on a white sandy bottom in seventy feet of water. Much of the wreckage can be found higher on the rocks, where it was tossed by more than a century of storm-generated waves. The wreck is on an island, so you need a boat to reach it.

Other shore wrecks such as the *Letitia*, the *A.W. Perry*, and the *Isleworth* offer potential to all levels of diving experience. Because they ran nose first onto the rocks, their bows lie broken up in the shallows while their sterns lie as deep as 130 feet: mute testimony to the uneven geological gradient that is typical of the area. These dives permit one to explore the deeper end of a wreck for a limited time, then, by working up the sloping cliff face, to explore the shallow end right up to ten feet, where safety decompression stops can be done while stabbing flounder or photographing marine life.

Offshore sites which require floating transportation, and which are well worth the charter fees, are wrecks as diverse as the *Daniel Steinman*, a steamship which sank in 1884 with a cargo of plate glass and bottles of ale, to the *Kolkhosnik*, a Russian freighter which scraped over Smithson Rock in 1942 and settled to the bottom with a load of war materiel such as barbed wire, munitions, truck parts, tires, and Grant tanks, all of which was headed for Archangel in order to bolster the Russian military machine. Dozens of other wrecks lie off the outer islands and submerged rocks waiting to be explored, all necessarily shallow due to the cause of sinking: running aground in fog or storm.

For those whose interests are more diverse, Halifax can undoubtedly satisfy your needs. Diving for bottles off old forts and ferry docks is incredibly rewarding: it is not uncommon to find bottles dating back to the early eighteen hundreds, or pharmaceutical bottles with names and addresses embossed on the glass. These areas also produce coins, ceramics, and clay pipes from all over the world.

Excited by food? In addition to game fish such as flounder, Halifax is noted for its abundance of ocean scallops. For a negligible fee you can buy a license that permits you to harvest a gallon of meat per day – that's after the critters have been shucked. Feast away.

The only negative side of diving off Halifax is the

strict law which prohibits catching lobsters, under threat of fine and confiscation of equipment. However, many fine restaurants can serve a dish of "bugs" that were caught fresh by local trappers.

For non-divers, and for divers during off-days or when the weather is uncooperative, Halifax has plenty to offer. The downtown maritime museum is worth a tour, as is the Citadel, a fort which sits high upon a hill in the center of town and which functions as a museum full of wonderful exhibits which are rich in local history. Watching the changing of the guard in their splendid red uniforms is like traveling through time to an earlier age.

And if you want to go out of town for a day, you can see the tidal bore as it rushes up the mud flats in nearby rivers; you can visit picturesque Peggy's Cove; or you can drive to Oak Island and become entranced by the treasure pit, reportedly dug in the late seventeen hundreds, and whose depths have yet to be plumbed and whose mystery has yet to be solved.

What's there to do in Halifax? Everything.

I organized annual two-week dive trips to Halifax in the 1970's and 1980's. I then passed the torch to Gene Peterson, who still continues the tradition.

I could write a book about the shipwrecks of Halifax, and my many adventures in diving on them. Perhaps some day I will.

Will the real deadeye please stand up?

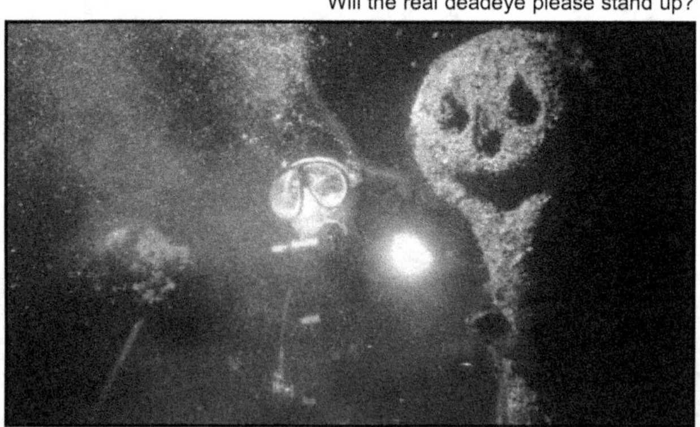

Sitting Ducks
Newfoundland's
Bell Island Wrecks

Many people think of Newfoundland as untrammeled wilderness, verdant forests furrowed by wild and scenic rivers, deep fjords sculpted from naked rock, and a rugged mountainous coastline. It fits all these descriptions, and more.

Newfoundland rises from the Atlantic Ocean with a craggy prominence that suggests a singular beauty beyond its rocky shores. Indeed, the island - which measures larger than the State of Maine, and which is Canada's easternmost extremity - consists largely of mountains and vast verdant forests. While backpackers and rock climbers prize the island for its topside terrain, divers find Newfoundland spectacular for its abundance of near-shore shipwrecks.

For centuries vessels have run aground on Newfoundland's seductive coastline: victims of strong and unpredictable currents, thick blankets of fog that often envelope the shore, and the uncertainties of navigating by dead reckoning. The seafloor is littered with thousands of wrecks of all kinds and ages. Many of these sites are largely unexplored or yet to be discovered. The frigid northern waters have spared from gross destruction these wood and metal monuments to man's arrogance and folly.

Perhaps the most interesting sites are four Allied iron-ore carriers that were torpedoed by German U-boats in Conception Bay. Because they are grouped together within sight of Bell Island, they are known collectively as the Bell Island wrecks.

My introduction to these wrecks was ominous, to say the least. The St. John's airport was in the throes of a blizzard as my plane landed on instruments in early April, on a runway that was invisible until the tarmac was close enough to touch. Snow fell all night long and throughout the next day, accompanied by high winds. I was happy to learn that the boat trip, planned for the first day of my arrival, was canceled. This afforded time to explore the local environs on foot. I took the opportunity to tramp the roads and mountain trails outside of town.

The rocky trails were icy. The vegetation was coated with rime. Snow blanketed the countryside like virgin fleece. Despite the swirling mist, the scenery was little less than spectacular as I negotiated a steep mountain trail under the protection of an eighteenth-century cannon. That night, comfortably ensconced in my warm and cozy bed-and-breakfast, I reviewed the tragic history of Newfoundland's involvement in World War Two.

St. John's was an important staging area for eastbound convoys about to cross the Atlantic, and a destination for westbound convoys that regrouped for coastwise passages southward along the American eastern seaboard. The Canadian Navy used the deep-water harbor as its convoy headquarters. St. John's was also an important fueling station for transatlantic shipping.

St. John's faces the broad reaches of the Atlantic. Bell Island is situated on the "back side" of St. John's: on the western flank of the peninsula. The island has long been a valuable source of iron ore, and sports one of the most productive mines in the world. The onset of hostilities in 1939 dramatically increased the strategic importance of raw iron: for the construction of ships, tanks, and guns that were needed to prosecute the war against the Nazis: Germany's fanatical political organization that was bent on world domination.

A defense garrison was deployed to the island to prevent enemy troops from landing and from sabotaging the entranceways to the mines. The Canadian Air Force patrolled the surrounding waters. When Germany finally focused its aggressive energies against the Bell Island facility, the attack came not from the sea or from the air, but from under water.

On September 5, 1942, a German U-boat crept around the southern end of Bell Island. Korvettenkapitan Rolf Ruggeberg, skipper of the *U-513*, peered through the sights of his periscope at two British freighters that floated placidly at their anchorage: the 5,454-ton *Saganaga*, and the 7,335-ton *Lord Strathcona*. Both unsuspecting vessels were laden with iron ore, and were awaiting escort by the Canadian Navy. The skippers were attending a pre-departure briefing ashore.

The water was calm and the air was clear. Bright sunshine illuminated the stationary targets. At 11:45 a.m., the *U-513* fired two torpedoes at the *Saganaga*. Both struck amidships in rapid succession, ripping the hull apart below the waterline. The freighter sank literally like the rock that she was carrying, in less than thirty seconds. There was no time to launch lifeboats or even to abandon ship. Quite the contrary, the *Saganaga* abandoned the crew instead of vice versa.

U-boats were the farthest thought from any British

Bathtub in the *Saganaga*.

seaman's mind. None was visible in the broad daylight. Witnesses suspected an internal explosion. Crewmembers of the *Lord Strathcona* launched lifeboats at once, and went to the rescue of their companions in the water, half a mile away.

Ruggeberg was more audacious than observant. He charged into the fray like a frenzied fox in a henhouse, but failed to notice the U-boat's proximity to his next intended victim. Cruising at a depth of 55 feet, the U-boat crashed into the bottom of the *Lord Strathcona* – much like a cartoon character running head first into an unseen post. The crushing of the conning tower was clearly heard by the German sailors. To break away from the hull, Ruggeberg ordered the ballast tanks flooded. The U-boat dived out of control, struck the bottom at 150 feet, and stuck there like a bug on a pin. The influx of seawater, leaking into the pressure hull through the direction-finder housing, made rapid release imperative. Positive buoyancy and rotating propellers soon freed the U-boat from the suction of the sand.

In his log, Ruggeberg wrote, "Start attack run on the ship which had collided with us." This is hardly a fair description. Blame cannot cast upon the anchored *Lord Strathcona* any more than a tree can be blamed for jumping in front of a car.

By this time – half an hour after the loss of the *Saganaga* – the *Lord Strathcona* lay completely abandoned. All hands were still in lifeboats, searching for survivors of the *Saganaga*. The *U-513* fired two torpe-

Rusticles surround a pressure gauge in the *Lord Strathcona*.

The *Rose Castle* was typical of the ore freighters that frequented Bell Island during the war. (Courtesy of Library and Archives Canada.)

does that struck the *Lord Strathcona* as she swung at anchor. Both torpedoes detonated, sinking the abandoned ore carrier in ninety seconds.

As no one was on board the *Lord Strathcona* at the time she sank, no fatalities occurred. But only fourteen men survived the sinking of the *Saganaga*. Twenty-nine others perished in the bold sneak attack. The men were either trapped inside and carried down to Davy Jones's Locker, or they drowned on the surface as they struggled to stay afloat in the frigid water.

The *U-513* made good its escape undetected.

Two months later – on November 2 – an identical repeat performance occurred. This time the attacker was the *U-518* (Kapitanleutnant Friedrich-Wilhelm Wissmann), and the victims were two more cargo carriers loaded with ore: the 7,803-ton *Rose Castle* (Canadian registry) and the 5,633-ton *P.L.M. 27* (a Free French ship under British registry; P.L.M. was the abbreviation for Paris-Lyon-Marseilles). Ironically, both vessels had been present during the previous attack: the *Rose Castle* was tied to the loading dock, while the *P.L.M. 27* lay at anchor barely a mile north of the torpedoed vessels. Perhaps the latter had been saved from an earlier fate by Ruggeberg's lack of attention and the U-boat's subsequent leakage.

The period of grace was now over for the *Rose Castle* and the *P.L.M. 27*.

By this time, Bell Island shipping was protected by

great alertness. A powerful searchlight swept Conception Bay with regularity that Wissmann first found annoying. Despite light rain and overcast, moonbeams speared through itinerant openings in the cloud cover. Wissmann dodged this combination of natural and artificial light with frustrating difficulty. After a while, however, he realized that he could take advantage of the searchlight's pendulum-like periodicity. Patiently he timed the sweeps, and learned that the duration of the cycle lasted for approximately ten minutes.

Wissmann waited for the searchlight beam to reach the end of its sweep. As soon as the beam changed direction, he attacked three pre-selected targets that were shrouded temporarily in darkness. The time was 3:30 a.m. Wissmann fired three torpedoes from the U-boat's forward tubes. The first one missed the anchored *Anna T*, passed by the fantail of the docked *Flyingdale*, and exploded against the wharf. The other two torpedoes struck the *Rose Castle*.

Wissmann turned the U-boat and fired a fourth torpedo from a stern tube at the *Rose Castle*. He continued turning until the third vessel was aligned in his sights. He fired a fifth torpedo at her from a forward tube. So quickly did the U-boat maneuver and fire that the last torpedo stuck the *P.L.M. 27* at the same moment that the first one struck the *Rose Castle*. The U-boat then "departed at full speed," leaving destruction in the wake of a perfectly executed attack sequence.

Both torpedoed ore carriers sank within minutes. Again there was no opportunity for crewmembers to launch lifeboats. Survivors barely had time to leap overboard. Emergency life rafts floated off the decks, offering places of safety for those who managed to stay afloat in the blackness of night. Cries for help went for the most part unheeded.

Corvettes were hampered in all their operations. They could not drop depth charges for fear of killing the men in the water, and they could not stop to rescue survivors for fear of being torpedoed by the U-boat.

They merely dashed back and forth in raging impotence.

Rousing from sleep by the loud detonations, civilian inhabitants of Bell Island put to sea in their fishing boats. They plucked some men out of the water, took others off rafts. Two survivors had severely broken legs; all the others were suffering from exposure. The fishing boats transported the survivors to a doctor's office on the island. Not until after dawn did the corvettes feel secure enough to assist in rescue operations. By that time, anyone who had not had the fortune to find a floating raft had perished from cold water immersion.

The death toll was substantial: twelve from the *P.L.M. 27*, twenty-eight from the *Rose Castle*.

Today, a granite monument stands on Bell Island in commemoration of the men who were killed during Germany's second attempt to conquer the world.

Sleet beating against the windowpanes brought me back to the present. Miraculously, the storm blew itself out to sea overnight. The second day of my weeklong excursion dawned bright and sunny and, considering the season, comparatively warm (above freezing).

Bell Island was located only a hopscotch away: less

Inside the *P.L.M. 27*, this grinding wheel must have been used to sharpen knives, chisels, and screwdrivers.

than half an hour by boat from the marina to any one of the four wrecks. The daily trips were easygoing and layback. The late morning departure still afforded plenty of time between dives to make excursions on the island to see the memorial, and to take leisurely hikes in uninhabited areas where graceful waterfalls drained the highlands and poured clear, cold freshwater into the sea. I even took a shower under one of the falls – while wearing my drysuit, of course.

All four wrecks sit upright. The hulls are intact except for torpedo damage. For example, the starboard bow of the *Rose Castle* is pierced by a perfectly round hole that measures twelve feet in diameter; around the perimeter, the plates are curled inward from the external explosion. The greatest noticeable damage to any of the wrecks is the collapse of the midship superstructures. Otherwise, the forecastles and poop decks are still extant (and penetrable), as are deckhouses and the lowest level of the superstructures.

In order of depth the wrecks are: *Rose Castle* (150 feet), *Lord Strathcona* (110 feet), *Saganaga* (105 feet), and *P.L.M. 27* (100 feet). The main deck of each wreck stands 40 above the bottom. Thus, one can swim along the deck of the *P.L.M. 27* at a depth of 60 feet, and explore the lower level of the *Rose Castle's* superstructure at 110 feet.

Experienced divers can venture inside to explore the compartments, corridors, deckhouses, and ore-filled holds. Many rooms are separated by wooden partitions that have been preserved by the prevalent cold water in which most wood-boring organisms do not thrive. In forecastle stowage areas I found hawsers whose natural fibers were still firm and solid.

The interiors are a wreck photographer's dream. Subject matter includes porcelain toilets and bathtubs, cutlery and dinnerware, wooden furniture and shelving, brass portholes with unbroken glass, radio equipment, electrical components, bitts, cargo booms, winches, windlasses, even a bronze steam whistle. Deck guns and shell casings lie scattered about. In the

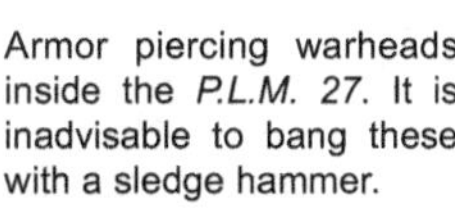

Armor piercing warheads inside the *P.L.M. 27*. It is inadvisable to bang these with a sledge hammer.

forecastle of the *P.L.M. 27* I found armor-piercing warheads.

A week is not long enough to explore these fascinating mementoes of the greatest war the world has ever known. The result of German arrogance is a peek into history that will provide wreck-divers with thrills for generations to come.

Newfoundland may not be the average person's ideal for a summer vacation, but it certainly has much to offer to those who are willing to stretch the envelope of diving destinations. Coastal waters boast the clarity of Caribbean reefs. During my stay, ambient light visibility never fell shorter than fifty feet – artificial lighting is necessary only for penetration.

I also took the time to swim through natural tunnels that bored through towering promontories. The hard-packed sandy bottom was alive with local denizens: sea anemones, starfish, sea urchins, mussels, kelp, several species of crabs, cod, flounder, snails, jellyfish, lobsters, and a wide variety of shellfish. All these forms of marine life can be found on the wrecks, whose decks are often indistinguishable from the seabed.

Perhaps the most spectacular and unanticipated treat is the sighting of an iceberg. In early summer, massive chunks of ice – some as tall as a ten-story building – calve off glaciers in the far north, and drift along Newfoundland's eastern shore. In late May and

June, visitors may spot icebergs floating in the surf, where the action of the waves causes them eventually to melt.

I have so far failed to mention only one major item of interest to divers: water temperature. In early April the bottom temperature was a brisk 28°! (That is degrees in Fahrenheit, not the Caribbean equivalent in centigrade.) I did not think that H_2O could be so cold in the liquid form – I thought it would have been solid at subfreezing temperatures. Fresh water freezes at 32° F. Seawater freezes at a lower temperature due to the presence of salt and other minerals.

And there was no thermocline!

When I jumped into the water, I felt as if someone had hit me in the forehead with a two-by-four. Within minutes my hands felt like blocks of ice, and my fingers were painfully cold and unworkable. After a dive and decompression I could not make a fist, so I had to climb up the boat ladder by hooking my elbows over the rungs. The only saving grace was the warm sun and a cup of steaming hot soup – which I did not drink but which I held in my hands.

Such frigid temperatures yield to the acceptable mid-50's in the summer, when the Gulf Stream veers close to land and mixes with the cold Labrador Current.

My advice? Dive in a drysuit, wear heavyweight long johns, add a sleeveless sweater for additional protection for the chest and vital organs, breathe nitrox to shorten the decompression penalty, carry an argon bottle for drysuit inflation, and grin and bear it.

But don't miss out on the Bell Island wrecks.

Diving Gets the Thumb

Or Rather, Two Thumbs Up

Place a left-handed mitten on a Michigan map between Lakes Michigan and Huron, and the thumb will cover an area of the lower State that is called appropriately the Thumb.

Only a couple of hour's drive along Route 53 north from Detroit, the State capital, the Thumb is a miniature Mecca for Great Lakes wreck-divers. Off the stretch of coast between Point Aux Barque and Port Huron – from the tip of the thumb south along the outer edge – rest the remains of dozens, perhaps scores, of beautifully preserved shipwrecks that still appear to be proceeding on surreal unfinished voyages.

For the casual diver or shipwreck connoisseur, diversity exists because of the sheer number of wrecks that litter the lakebed: vessels from the nineteenth and twentieth centuries, hulls constructed of wood and iron, propelling power from wind and steam, depth ranging from 35 feet and descending ever deeper. Depending upon a person's choice and level of experience, dives can be shallow or deep, long or short.

At the shallow end of this shipwreck paradise lies the *Chicamauga*. She foundered one mile north of Harbor Beach in 1919, then was moved to a spot east of Harbor Beach harbor. The wreck now lies half a mile from shore in 35 feet of clean fresh water. The hull of this schooner is contiguous and longer than a football field. The shallow depth offers ample bottom time for extended exploration of the wooden remains. Because the lake is not a marine environment, the wrecks are not encrusted by marine fouling organisms (coral and barnacles), and the wood is not decomposed by wood-boring mollusks such as teredos (which are found only in salt water).

The *Glenorchy* is a steel-hulled steamship that sank in 1924 after colliding with the *Leonard B. Miller*. The hull is 365 feet long, and rests some ten miles off Harbor Beach. Lying 120 feet deep, the wreck falls within the suggested depth range for recreational diving, yet offers a challenge for those with a venturesome vein. Large portions of the hull are intact, beckoning to divers to penetrate into the cold, dark interior. Guidelines and two lights are recommended.

The *Chicamauga's* and the *Glenorchy's* pristine state of preservation exemplifies that found throughout the Great Lakes. Wood is so well preserved that the grain is often evident. Steel shows signs of oxidation but retains its structural stability.

The summer thermocline fluctuates between 30 and 60 feet. Wetsuits are suitable only for shore and shallow dives, where the temperature may climb to a comfortable 70°. Below the thermocline the temperature rarely rises above the low 40's: drysuit diving for all but the hardiest.

Visibility averages between ten and thirty feet; it will be worse after a storm has stirred the brown bottom sediments. One distinct advantage to diving off the Thumb: no current.

Divers wanting to explore more than wrecks will not be disappointed. The rugged rocky lakeshore offers cavelike recesses that have been eroded from limestone. There are no long, sinuous tunnels in which to get lost, nor do the holes ever leave the light zone. Many of these openings can be snorkeled.

Grindstones – once the main product of Grindstone City – are strewn across the bottom where they were dumped by previous generations in which environmental awareness was lacking. A grindstone is a stone disk that is turned on an axle; it was used to grind, polish, and sharpen tools. These grindstones may measure more than three feet in diameter.

The more popular wrecks are buoyed, and their locations are published in books about local diving.

Boaters are cautioned to tie their boats to the buoys in order to protect the wrecks from grapnel damage.

All this and more is available in a lovely forested area that lacks metropolitan crowding.

Of my top ten all-time favorite shipwrecks in the world, two reside on the bottomlands of the Great Lakes: the *Dunderberg* and the *Florida*. Each presents particular appeal and possesses features that are scarce among shipwrecks. Coincidentally, both vessels lie within fifty miles of each other off the Thumb in Lake Huron. Their hulls were constructed of wood, and both sank in the nineteenth century, but there the similarities end. The *Dunderberg* was a schooner of antique design, the *Florida* a steamship of advanced technology.

In the ocean, wood and metal would long since have yielded their original form and structure to the corrosive chemical environment. Yet the cold fresh water of the Great Lakes has done an admirable job of extending the life of man's ephemeral creations. The process of deterioration is inevitable, but its speed is reduced by the absence of marine boring mollusks, wood digesting bacteria, and destructive oxidizing agents. Shipwrecks abide in the Inland Sea like nowhere else in the world.

The freshwater bottomlands are largely free of macroscopic life forms. Green, velvety algae sometimes veneer rocks and wrecks, and tiny zebra mussels are seen in growing populations. The lucky diver might spot a burbot or an eel, possibly even a crayfish. Otherwise the sites are untenanted.

Of the thousands of shipwrecks that adorn the five lakebeds, the *Dunderberg* and *Florida* are exceptional in their state of preservation and in the spectacle they present to the shipwreck connoisseur. Upon returning from my first dive to each of these unique sites, I instantly proclaimed that each was among the most fascinating wrecks I had ever explored: by dint of historic significance as well as photogenic quality. Neither wreck has lost its place in my heart or in my hierarchy of distinction.

The *Dunderberg* was only one year old – and the Civil War only three years ended – when she collided at night with the propeller *Empire State*. The date of the disaster was August 13, 1868. The stem of the *Empire State* clove a V-shaped hole in the *Dunderberg's* hull. The three-masted schooner sank within minutes, taking one passenger and 40,000 bushels of corn down to 155 feet. The *Empire State* rescued the crew and the other passengers.

If ever a wreck fits the fictitious image that Hollywood promotes to the masses, this is the one. The hull breach, a few broken planks, and the broken masts and rigging are all that distinguish the *Dunderberg* from a movie set in a pirate flick or a museum piece in a protected wharf. The wreck sits upright like a ship in dry dock awaiting minor repairs. Metal parts are untarnished, the planks are unblemished, and the grain in the wood is clearly in evidence. A light layer of silt and algae are all that mar the façade of this picture perfect shipwreck, and a dust brush is all that is needed to prepare the wreck for show.

What makes the *Dunderberg* a wreck apart from others is not the intact hull, the holystoned decks, the protruding bowsprit, or the proliferation of deadeyes that line the bulwarks and litter the lakebed – many Great Lakes shipwrecks afford similar affectations – but the artistic ornamentation. The *Dunderberg* was a Cadillac among schooners of ancient vintage, possessing a beautifully molded hull and lovingly carved upperworks.

The cathead is a prime example. This stout wooden beam is a functional device which is employed in raising the anchor. The bottom of the *Dunderberg's* cathead is ornately carved with connecting curlicue designs that resemble leaves: the equivalent of chrome trim or painted detail on a fancy sport car.

Another example is the bitt on the forecastle head. Instead of a solid drum or a plain spindle of wood, the *Dunderberg's* bitt entails a decorative pattern of radiating grooves: the precursor to magnesium wheels.

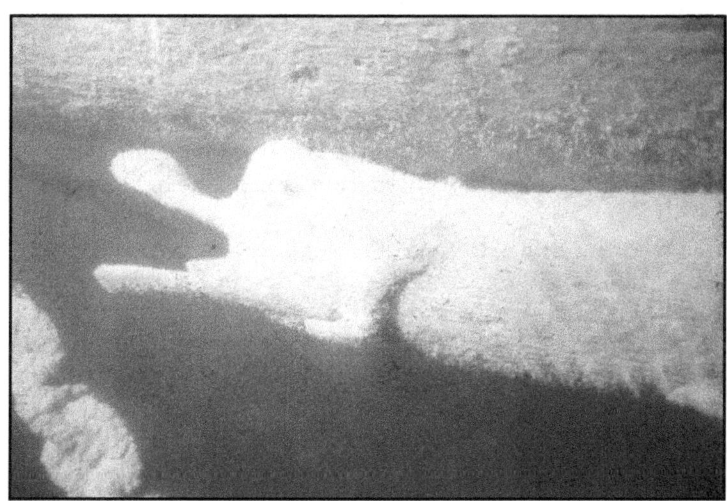

But the pièce de résistance is the fabulous figurehead and elaborately carved trailboards. No simple hood ornament, the figurehead is kind of a toothless alligator with legs like a dachshund, and which is sculpted from a single block of wood. The alligator's tail morphs into a pair of delicately wrought trailboards that grace either side of the cutwater for a length of eight feet. The foliage motif of the cathead is continued with twisted trunks of vines, twigs, leaves, and graven birds feeding on clusters of grapes.

These uncommon embellishments are reminiscent of archaic Greek marble: unnecessary adornments which add pure yet simple elegance to an otherwise workaday vessel, and the addition of which demonstrates both the craftsmanship of the builder and the undisguised pride of the owner.

The "loss" of the *Dunderberg* represents a one-of-a-kind "find" for present-day wreck-divers who can now observe and appreciate the careful construction of sailing vessels of yesteryear, when shipbuilders were artisans in addition to being woodworkers. We can be thankful today that the *Dunderberg* sank in the halcyon days of her youth, instead of living to a ripe old age and being ignominiously chopped up for firewood.

The *Florida* is a vessel of a different breed: a package freighter built in 1889, and sunk by collision with the *George W. Roby*, on May 20, 1897. Once again, yesteryear's loss is today's gain. The attraction of the wreck is not its aesthetic appeal, but the sights to see and the challenge of exploration: for it lies at a depth of 195 feet.

Bottom times are short, decompressions are long, and the water is always cold: 38° in the middle of August! Despite these disincentives and commonplace construction, the wreck is amazingly "shipshape" in appearance and nonpareil in its own right. The hull sits upright and is intact except for the stern, where it was neatly sliced in two by the other steamer's stem. The collapse of the stern section is fortuitous for divers because it exposed the engine and its magnificent gauge panel. The brass gauges are highly polished, and the lettering on the faceplates is eminently legible.

Lying in the debris field is the ship's bell. Nearby is a brass capstan cover whose black paint is as shiny as it was on the day it was applied, and on which is stamped the vessel's name, year of construction, and the builder's name and address. There is no doubt about this wreck's identity!

Forward of the cut is the deckhouse. The after cabin contains a monstrous boiler, complete with attendant

piping and pressure gauges, several of which have fallen onto the wooden deck. A pair of unbroken sight tubes – to monitor the water level in the boiler – are exposed.

The forward cabin contains some of the navigational stores: running lights, Fresnel lenses, kerosene lanterns, and spare glass globes. They were originally stowed on shelves, but now they lie in a jumbled heap, like refuse in a ship chandlery that has gone out of business. One such lamp stands on the deck outside the doorway – placed there by a thoughtful diver for visitors to admire.

As if that were not fascinating enough, an emergency fire axe still resides in its holders on the outside of the forward partition.

The forecastle possesses its own items of interest, the primary one being a capstan and a duplicate cover of the one found in the after debris field, complete with the stamps of identification. Two iron anchors lie adjacent to the starboard bulwark. The stem is sheathed in iron to enable the vessel to plow through ice without incurring damage to the hull. Draft marks in Roman numerals grace the iron sheath.

In between the forecastle and the deckhouse stretch two hundred feet of cargo holds. Penetration is conveniently straightforward because the hatch covers are absent. One can enter through a hatchway at either end, and negotiate each successive hold to the opposite end. Intermediate hatchways allow for emergency egress, and also let in diffuse ambient light. The soft green glow that enters through the hatchways is a dim but constant beacon that illuminates the way in front.

One can also drop down through a second set of hatchways into the lower cargo deck. Here it is spooky and the darkness is nearly absolute. Both the upper and lower holds are crammed with packaged freight. And here lies the wreck's greatest allure.

Some dry goods were packed in barrels whose staves burst outward when the contents solidified and expanded. Other merchandise was packed in sealed cans or metal canisters whose sides bent inward due to the pressure. Narrow wooden boxes are stacked like cordwood. Enameled metal pails retain their blue or white colors. Washbasins are nested together one inside the other. Handcarts lie about haphazardly, where they were flung in violence when the *Florida* slammed against the sandy bottom.

Century-old items – the daily commodities of an earlier generation – are strewn throughout the capacious holds with an incredible lack of disarray. One could spend hours sifting through miscellaneous cargo, reading the labels on containers, and examining the contents.

The *Florida* has much – too much – to offer the inquisitive diver.

These two extraordinary shipwrecks transcend the overall essence of wreck-diving. Wreck-divers are adventurers who explore the past by frequenting the remnants of maritime history. The only tangible parts of that history that extend into the present are dissociated artifacts that are displayed in museums, and shipwrecks and their cargoes that reside in the watery realm.

The *Dunderberg* and the *Florida* proffer quintessential attractions that should entice every wreck-diver who is worth his salt – even though the surrounding water is fresh.

Waterspouts formed and deformed while we were preparing to dive. We dived anyway.

Two Freighters
John Morgan and Lillian Luckenbach

Off the coast of Virginia lies a plethora of shipwrecks, docked underwater like battered antique cars after a maritime version of a demolition derby. There are wooden hulls and steel hulls, sailing ships and steamships, tankers and freighters, fishing trawlers and passenger vessels, barges and galleons, tugboats and gunboats, submarines and U-boats, even American and German battleships.

Amid this junk yard of rotting and rusting hulls, two of the most fascinating wrecks to explore are the freighters *John Morgan* and *Lillian Luckenbach*: tragic remnants of the bloody days of World War Two, when German U-boats lurked off the eastern seaboard to prey upon unsuspecting merchantmen. Due to the concentration of shipping in the mouth of the Chesapeake Bay, where convoys formed and waited for armed escorts to see them through the gauntlet of mines and torpedoes, accidents abounded.

Came the night when the *Lillian Luckenbach* was headed out to sea. It was March 26, 1943, and she was traveling in single file through the mine-swept channel when out of the darkness loomed the unlighted hull of an inbound steamship, the *Cape Henlopen*. The two steel titans came together with a bone-jarring crash and a sheet of sparks that showered their decks. The *Cape Henlopen* caught fire and drifted away, but she was not holed and she was in no immediate danger of sinking. The fires were soon extinguished, and the vessel drifted onto a shoal on which she grounded.

Lillian Luckenbach. (Official U.S. Coast Guard photo.)

The *Lillian Luckenbach* was badly damaged. Her hull was stove in and she was taking on water faster than her pumps could eject it. Shortly after midnight, about forty-five minutes after the collision, the gallant ship heeled over onto her starboard side, and sank. There were no casualties.

The depth of water given at the time was 80 feet. In the years since her demise, tidal currents have scoured the sandy bottom around the rusty remains, so that the wreck now rests at an average depth of 90 to 95 feet, with deeper washouts sometimes appearing. The wreck was never salvaged, nor was it demolished, even though it presented a hazard to navigation. Instead, an extra dogleg was placed in the mine-swept channel, forcing subsequent wartime shipping to zigzag around the wreckage.

Today, the *Lillian Luckenbach* is a seductive dive site: festooned with anemones and schools of bait fish, visited often by ocean sunfish, and explored regularly by divers who drive hundreds of miles to see this wartime relic – and her relics of war. For she is still heavily laden with the guns that she never fired, and the cargo that was never salvaged.

The gun tub in the bow lies upside down; the enterprising diver can crawl inside and see the breech and the barrel and the brass hand wheels, uncluttered by filter-feeding marine organisms because they cannot siphon nutrients out of water with such little flow. Abaft the peak lie the kingposts and cargo booms,

Shown on the opposite page are parts of the general wartime cargo that are exposed on the *Lillian Luckenbach*. From top to bottom: a gun shell canister, a truck axle with dual wheels, and an aircraft engine.

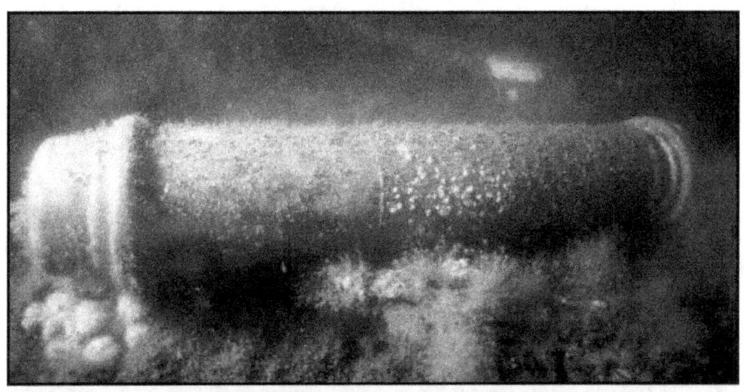

Two machine gun barrels protrude from this aircraft wing on the *Lillian Luckenbach*.

arranged like a drop of giant Pickup Sticks. Then come perfectly preserved tires in a wide variety of tread patterns, truck chassis, tires, heavy-duty axles, tires, airplanes, and more tires. Everywhere there are tires.

The *Lillian Luckenbach* was carrying airplanes when she went down, but the thin aluminum fuselages have long since corroded away, leaving behind the disarticulated sections as if they had been carried as spare parts. Among the debris, the observant diver will notice engines, oil filters, air coolers, and an occasional wing. One wing still has the barrels of two fifty-caliber machines protruding from its leading edge.

The superstructure lies spread out across the sand for fifty feet or more. It is here that the lucky diver will find portholes and lobsters and, for those who like to dive with a speargun, giant tautog that will feed more than one large family several times over. With a wreck that is nearly a city block in length, there is more to see than the average diver can cover during the course of a single dive – or many dives, for that matter.

Two months after the *Lillian Luckenbach* took her final plunge, the *John Morgan* set out on her maiden voyage, carrying valuable war materiel to the beleaguered Russian front. When she reached the new dogleg around the wreckage of the *Lillian Luckenbach*, the

The *John Morgan's* sister ship *John Brown.*

outbound convoy found itself sliding alongside an inbound convoy that consisted of only two ships: the tanker *Montana* and her escort. All vessels were blacked out due to wartime restrictions. The *John Morgan* and the *Montana* met at the dogleg; each turned, one inside the other, but not sharply enough. The steel hulls scraped along each other in what might have been a glancing blow had not each of the vessels been carrying the cargo that she had.

The *Montana's* tanks were filled with high-octane aviation fuel. The forward cargo holds of the *John Morgan* were packed with more than 1,300 *tons* of explosives. Sparks ignited the aviation fuel, and the *Montana* burst into flames – which almost instantly leaped to the *John Morgan* and detonated her cargo of TNT, cannon ammunition, and smokeless powder. The resulting explosion vaporized the *John Morgan* forward of the wheelhouse, killed practically everyone on board, and blew out the bridge windows of an escort vessel half a mile away. The freighter sank immediately. The tanker was eventually salvaged.

From that tragedy has come another of wreck-diving's great experiences, for in addition to the munitions that went up in flames, there still remains the cargo stowed in the after compartments: more than a quarter million high-explosive shells, two million 50-caliber cartridges, 39 *tons* of machine guns, 48 Ford trucks, 20 Caterpillar tractors, 240 motorcycles, 140 Willy's jeeps, and 10 Valentine tanks. The tanks are a magnificent sight to see. Some sit upright in the bottom of the blasted-out holds, with turrets and guns intact, while others lie on their sides with their treads blown off.

Then there are the airplanes – P-39 Airacobras – not packed in crates and ready for assembly, but spread across the bottom as if they had been shot out of the sky: an engine here, a propeller there, the remains of an instrument panel bent and crushed under a collapsed hull plate.

Don't expect to find machine guns packed in cosmoline, either. They are undoubtedly buried under the shifting sand, and haven't been seen in years.

With all the ammunition on the bottom, the *John Morgan* more closely resembles a hastily abandoned battlefield than a wreck site. And that is its attraction.

So which wreck should you dive the next time you visit Virginia Beach? The *John Morgan* has tanks and munitions and is mostly broken open. The *Lillian Luckenbach* is more nearly intact, has an immense debris field, and is largely ignored due to interest in the *John Morgan.* The wrecks lie only a mile apart, so it's easy to hit them both on the same day.

On the other hand, if you like to get oriented on the first dive, then do your serious exploration on the second, you'll have to make a choice. Take the rational approach and flip a coin.

Then again, there are always overnight trips.

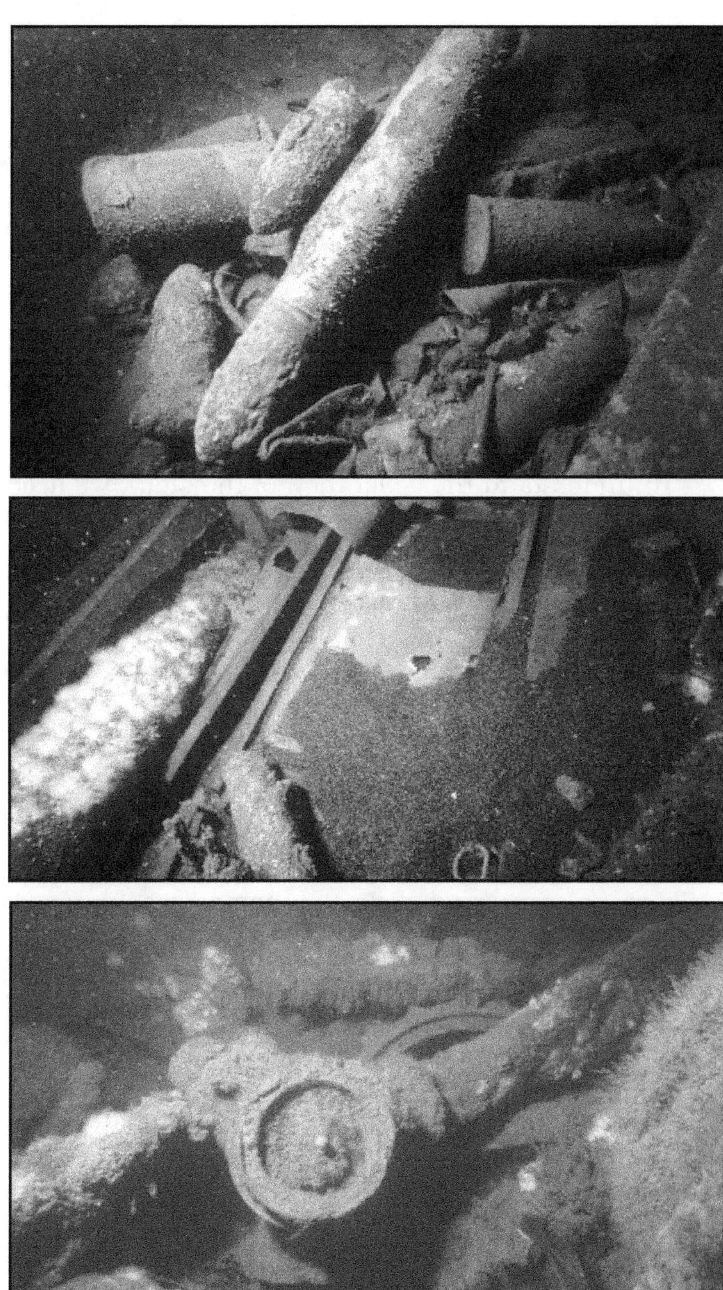

Miraflores
Identification of an Unknown Freighter

This story goes back fifteen years. That is how long it took for the events that began in the summer of 1992 to run full circle.

To understand the generation of the story, we need to go back even farther: to 1986. That was when Homer Pratt, skipper of the *Ursula*, accidentally ran over a previously unknown wreck site southeast of Cape May, New Jersey. That autumn he took a group of divers to the wreck, in 160 feet of water. The divers were delighted to find the remains of an ancient screw steamer that was loaded with artifacts. They named the wreck Homer's Hot Spot in honor of the finder and the trove of artifacts that they recovered from the site.

Despite subsequent sporadic trips to the wreck, Homer's Hot Spot remained unidentified for the next six years. Then, on July 26, 1992, Mike Edge recovered the builder's plaque on which the name was stamped: *Charles Morand*. The *Charles Morand* sank on July 26, 1890 after colliding with the schooner *Zacheus Sherman*. Full particulars of the discovery and loss are related in *Shipwrecks of New Jersey: South*.

As chance would have it, Gene Peterson had a charter scheduled on the *Down Deep* three days after Homer's Hot Spot was identified. I was signed up for the charter. When we arrived at the Cape May dock on the morning of July 29, we had no intention of going to the *Charles Morand*, because the location had not been disclosed. However, Bob Meimbreese, skipper of the *Down Deep*, informed us that he had recently obtained some wreck numbers from Jim Bowen, skipper of the lobster boat *Wayward*, and that the *Charles Morand* was among them. He asked us if we wanted to go there instead of to our intended destination.

It took only the blink of an eye for us to change our plans. Once on site, Gene and I went down first to set the hook. We then circumnavigated the wreck. Visibility was about thirty feet ambient, so we had a good look at the site. We exchanged shrugs when we returned to the anchor line. Although the depth was right, the wreck did not fit the description that we had been given of the *Charles Morand*. It was obvious to both of us that this wreck belonged to a much later era: no earlier than World War One, and possibly as late as World War Two.

We had discovered a previously undived shipwreck!

Because we found no significant artifacts, I christened it Bob's Cold Spot. As other divers started to visit the wreck, it collected a host of aliases: the Unknown Freighter, Dudley's Freighter, and the Ice Cream Cone.

Artifacts were recovered on subsequent trips, but none that helped to identify the wreck. And there matters remained for the next two years.

On July 4, 1994, I was diving with Tom Packer on Bob's Cold Spot when I spotted a dark shape some fifty feet off the port side of the wreck. I swam across the white sandy bottom to investigate. What I found was a disarticulated chunk of wreckage that was shrouded in fishing nets. Under the netting I saw several portholes and, after close examination, the helm and brass stand. I had discovered the wheelhouse wreckage!

I signaled frantically with my light. Tom saw the wagging beam and raced across the open sand to my side. I showed him the helm stand and portholes. He was ecstatic.

Because the wreck was so far offshore, we had planned to make only one deep dive, then come inshore to dive on a shallow wreck which had been discovered several weeks before. Eight minutes into the repetitive dive I found a brass stencil which I held up to the light, and read "S.S. CLEOPATRA." Positive identification!

I had written about the 1899 collision between the *Cleopatra* and the *Crystal Wave* in *Shipwrecks of Delaware and Maryland.* Neither wreck had been located at the time of publication, in 1990. I updated the relevant chapters when I revised the book in 2002.

To return to Bob's Cold Spot, which we did the following day, I dived with John Moyer because Tom had to work. After hooking into the wreck, I led John to the wheelhouse wreckage. We did what we could to free the stand from the wreckage, and ran a guideline to the anchor line. Gene Peterson and Lynn DelCorio went down next, secured two 500-pound liftbags to the helm stand, and inflated them. The positive buoyancy broke the stand free from the surrounding debris, and raised it about ten feet off the bottom, but there it hung – held by the net like a bug in a spider web. The addition of another liftbag did not break the stand free. They tied a sisal line to the stand, and reeled the line to the boat's anchor line. After decompressing, they brought the line to the boat so there was a direct line to the stand.

John and I had not planned to make a repetitive deep dive. But we certainly were not about to leave the stand where it was hanging. We followed the guideline to the bottom. I took photographs while John secured a safety line to the stand. John backed away. I circled the shroud of netting, cutting one strand at a time. When I cut the last strand that entangled the helm, the stand exploded toward the surface like a Titan missile launched from a nuclear submarine. It took all of us to haul the heavy stand onto the boat.

Gene expressed an interest in displaying the helm in his dive shop, Atlantic Divers. In fact, as if in prescience, he had mentioned that to me on the evening prior to the trip on which I found the stand, when I slept at his house. I thought his shop was a prime location for public display. So he took the helm home, cleaned it, and stood it prominently in the shop for all his customers to see.

I entertained the hope that the cover of the stand had writing that would lead to the identification of the wreck, the way the helm stand that I recovered in 1973 from the *Ioannis P. Goulandris* had done. When Gene cleaned the stand, he did find lettering stamped on the cover: "John Hastie Co. Ltd, Patented Greenock," and a serial number: "2705".

Unfortunately, the stamping referred to no ships that were known to have been lost in the area. And that is where matters stood for thirteen years.

In 2007, Gene decided to use the Internet to conduct research about the manufacturer of the helm stand. He quickly ascertained that the John Hastie Company was located in Scotland. From the Glasgow University Archives, he learned that the company furnished steering gear to local shipbuilders. As steering gear technology evolved, the company used the same serial number three times: once for screw gear, once for steam gear, and once for hydraulic gear.

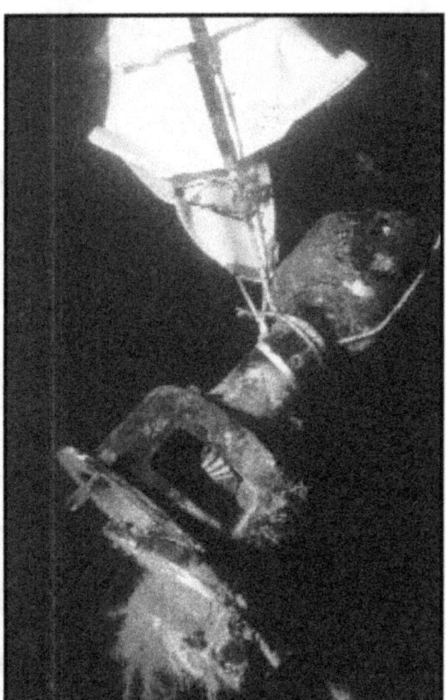

Left: The helm stand tethered to the bottom by fishing net. Below: the helm stand cap with the manufacturer's name and location.

The dates for the screw steering gear were too early for the wreck, while the dates for the hydraulic steering gear were too late. That left the steam steering gear, the item in question having been shipped to Swan Hunter & Wigham in 1920, where two sister ships were then under construction: the *St. Mary* and the *Miraflores.*

The *St. Mary* burned and sank in the Mississippi River in the 1950's, and was subsequently scrapped. The *Miraflores* disappeared without a trace after departing Haiti on February 14, 1942. She never reached her destination, which was New York City. The fate of her thirty-four hands was unknown; they were reported missing and presumed dead.

Gene learned that secondary German sources credited the *U-432*, Kapitanleutnant Heinz-Otto Schultze, with sinking the *Miraflores* on February 19, 1942, in a grid square that approximated the location of Bob's Cold Spot.

Hats off to Gene for a fine piece of research!

The U.S. Navy kept records of all vessels that were lost or attacked in what was known during the war as the Eastern Sea Frontier, an operational area that extended from Maine to northern Florida, and to a distance of one hundred miles from shore. The *Miraflores* did not appear in the war diary of the ESF. This

Miraflores. (From the collection of Gene Peterson.)

accounts for how I missed the *Miraflores* when I wrote *Track of the Gray Wolf*. The ESF war diary was my primary source of information relating to vessels that were lost in the area.

After the war, the Allies established an Assessment Committee to comb German records for the purpose of establishing which U-boat sank which Allied vessel, and which Allied warships and aircraft should receive credit for sinking which U-boat. Again, there was no mention of the *Miraflores* in American records.

This gave me pause to wonder what latter-day German researchers thought they knew that the Assessment Committee had missed. Since the National Archives has microfilms of U-boat deck logs, I decided to look at the log of the *U-432* for the period in question. What I found added ambiguity to an already puzzling story.

According to the records, Schultze sank the *Olinda* off the Virginia Capes on the night of February 18, 1942. The name is actually typed in the deck log. Schultze knew for certain the name of the vessel because the skipper was taken aboard the U-boat for interrogation. Captain Benemond was then released. The USS *Dallas* rescued the entire crew after they spent an uncertain night at sea. The wreck of the *Olinda* has not been found.

Eight hours later, Schultze noted in his log an attack on a 4,000-ton merchant vessel. No name was given. It is this entry on which the credit for sinking the *Miraflores* is based. Yet somehow the Allied Assessors overlooked this entry. On the other hand, the Assessors credited Schultze with sinking the *Norlavore* six days later, when there is no log entry to corroborate it, simply because he was in the area in which the Assessors believed the *Norlavore* sank with all hands.

The speculation that is currently in vogue adds the *Miraflores* tonnage to Schultze's credit, but subtracts the *Norlavore* tonnage: 2,158 tons instead of 2,677 tons.

So who was right – the contemporary Assessors or

recent German researchers? I dislike taking sides in a debate that is shrouded by so much opacity. But if I had to render an expert opinion, I would give Schultze credit for sinking the *Miraflores*, and take away credit for sinking the *Norlavore.*

No matter who is right or who is wrong, I don't think it mattered to the thirty-four men who lost their lives in the sinking of the *Miraflores*, or to the twenty-eight men who died in the sinking of the *Norlavore*. When all is said and done, human lives are more important than tonnage statistics. That is a cross that the Nazis refused to bear in their bid for world domination.

On a personal level, I wish that Gene had found this information a year earlier, before I published *The Fuhrer's U-boats in American Waters*. Then I could have incorporated this previously unknown story in the text and appendices.

It only goes to show that shipwreck research is never-ending.

Never-ending is right. Gene continued his research on the Miraflores, *and uncovered some interesting facts. The* Miraflores *measured 270 feet in length. She was owned by the Standard Fruit Company. Her cargo usually consisted of tropical fruits such as bananas, coconuts, and cashews, which she transported from Central American ports to New Orleans. After the U.S. entry into World War Two, Captain Charles Thompson, master, was ordered to proceed to Haiti for additional cargo, thence to New York City. This change in orders placed the* Miraflores *on a converging course with a German torpedo.*

According to Gene's research, at 3:18 a.m. "Schultze positioned his submarine perpendicular to the little fruit ship steaming north and fired two torpedoes. Both struck the freighter with a united explosive power. The first torpedo struck forward of the wheelhouse cutting the ship in two which left the bow intact. The second followed striking amidship obliterating the stern forward of the aft deck house. It is probable that this enormous explosion caused the S.S. Miraflores *to sink within a few minutes. The possibility of the crew escaping the doomed sinking ship was nil. Had anyone survived the tremendous blast, the icy cold water and confusion in darkness diminished all hopes of escape to less than a few minutes. Hypothermia would spare no one in such an inhospitable frigid sea so far from land. No distress call could be made due to the direct and devastating blast near the bridge that probably stunned or killed all officers and crew in that proximity instantly."*

The U-432 *suffered a similar fate a year later. "After sinking the* Miraflores, *Schultze and the* U-432 *continued to plunder the American shipping route. The U-boat torpedoed the* Azalea City *farther off the New Jersey coast on February 21 and then the* Marore *off North Carolina before crossing the Atlantic to La Pallice to resupply. Three more successful patrols under Schultze were made by the* U-432 *on convoys in the north Atlantic.*

"On March 11, 1943, the U-432 *was detected by ASDIC of the Free French corvette* Aconit. *The* U-432 *success was soon to end. The crew under the new command of Hermann Eckhardt was celebrating the sinking of HMS* Harvester *of convoy HX-228. Failing to observe the corvette, the* U-432 *was taken off guard and machine gunned killing several crew including Eckhardt.* U-432 *was then accidentally rammed during a boarding attempt and sank. Twenty-six crewmembers were lost and 20 were captured, interrogated and then spent the remainder of the war as POWs."*

After commanding the U-432, *Schultze took command of the* U-849. *On November 25, 1943, the* U-849 *sank with all hands in the South Atlantic, by depth charges that were dropped from an American B-24 Liberator.*

Gene related other parts of the story via his online dive shop newsletter:

"The wreck is 53 miles southeast of Cape May in 165 feet of water. In 1992 Bill Dumeze the captain of the red hulled clammer Arlene Snow *ran over a snag while fishing. He contacted Jim Bowen an avid wreck fisher and*

the two left Cape May inlet following only a compass bearing to the wreck site. Jim believed this was going to be some wild goose chase because Bill had recorded no loran numbers. After four long hours steaming at 12 knots to the middle of nowhere Captain Bill told Jim to slow the boat down and follow his bearings as he scanned the bottom finder. After what seemed to be a convoluted course of bearing changes over a period of a half hour, Bill shouted to drop a buoy. Jim Bowen looked over Bill's shoulders as a large spike appeared on the screen that looked like an ice cream cone with a sprinkle of jimmies. These were in fact fish hovering over the virgin wreck. Jim was amazed that any one could find a wreck scanning a depth recorder with no land bearings. Bill explained that clammers and scallopers know the bottom of the ocean well spending 99% of their time looking at the depth recorder searching for their harvest. Jim gave the wreck its first nick name the Ice Cream Cone."

Gene advertised the identification on several war memorial sites. He professed his interest in contacting surviving family members. Eventually he made contact with one former crewmember, with a grandson of the vessel's carpenter, and with a great-granddaughter of another crewmember.

The former crewmember was Walter Autry. He joined the merchant marine service at the age of 17. He served aboard the Miraflores *for a year in the capacity of a fireman. He left the* Miraflores *in 1940 in order to join the U.S. Navy. He attended diesel school in 1941, then spent the war aboard naval vessels that operated in the Pacific Theater.*

Gene sent Autry a piece of wood that he recovered from the wreck. This piece of wood is now Autry's most cherished possession.

David Shields, grandson of the vessel's carpenter, Willard Ebanks, called Gene on the phone and chatted about the grandfather he never knew. Gene sent him a piece of wood, too.

Karen Magill's great-grandfather was John Jule Brockerville. He was born on October 24, 1889, on St.

Pierre (a small island off the coast of Newfoundland but owned by France). The family moved to Newfoundland shortly after young John was born.

Gene struck up a correspondence with her, and sent her a packet that contained an account of the wreck's discovery and subsequent identification.

Karen wrote to Gene, "I am overwhelmed and in tears looking at the photographs and reading the stories within the links you have so graciously provided to me. I cannot express how happy my family will be to see these!

"My great-grandfather, John Jule Brockerville, was born on October 24, 1889 on an island called St. Pierre (a small island owned by France, just off the coast of Newfoundland). He was named after his father, Jean Gilles Broqueville, who was born in Cancale, France on October 20, 1863 and was lost at sea 19th of December 1892. Shortly afterward, his mother moved from the island over to Newfoundland, to a small fishing village called Roundabout, where my grandfather Gregory Joseph Brockerville was born (August 20, 1912). The family eventually re-settled in Lawn, Newfoundland, my

Karen Magill furnished these family photos of her grandfather.

family's hometown. Lawn is located on the very southern tip of Newfoundland, on the Burin Peninsula, in Placentia Bay. My grandfather also was a sailor in WWII, but for the Canadian Navy.

"During World War I, Newfoundland was still under British rule and was not yet part of Canada. My great-grandfather enlisted with the Royal Navy and served on various ships throughout the war. I have attached his naval records, which I obtained from over in the U.K. His enlistment papers show his place of birth as Marystown, which is a town near our village in Newfoundland. I can only assume it was easier to enlist and get payment if you stated your birthplace as British (Newfoundland) and not French (the island St. Pierre). He survived the Great War and returned home to Newfoundland.

"When World War II broke out, he was too old to serve, so enlisted in the Merchant Marines instead. . . . I can't begin to express to you how much all of your information and photographs are going to mean to my family. My second cousin, Earl Brockerville, in particular, has been trying for years to obtain information on his grandfather and, quite frankly, this information is going to make him a very happy man. Both Earl and myself are very avid history and genealogy buffs and, boy oh boy, I feel like I just hit the jackpot! Again, I can't thank you enough."

As Gene wrote so prophetically, "The human story of shipwrecks often exceeds our expectations. The misery that was suffered in order to maintain our freedom should never be forgotten."

Every year, Gene organizes a memorial dive to the Miraflores. *After a moment of silence, he places flowers over the wreck site in honor of the missing crewmen who sacrificed their lives in the cause of freedom.*

Amen.

Sharks and Shipwrecks

Malchace and Manuela

In the dire days of World War Two, German U-boats sank hundreds of innocent merchant vessels off the American eastern seaboard. Many of these encrusted remains have become popular dive sites. Two wrecks that have intrigued me the most were marked on the chart as the *Malchacc* and the *Manuela*. These freighters were similar in appearance, were torpedoed two months apart, and lay near each other off Ocracoke Island, North Carolina. Undived, they were ripe for exploration.

On April 9, 1942, the *Malchace* was torpedoed without warning by the *U-160*. The explosion started a fire and shrouded the deck with clouds of steam. One seaman leaped overboard in a panic, and drowned. The U-boat circled the freighter as the remaining crewmembers launched lifeboats and rafts. The men barely had time to abandon ship before the Nazi submarine launched another torpedo at the stationary target. The second blast breached the engine room and number three hold. The *Malchace* listed to port and settled slowly by the stern. The U-boat submerged, leaving the survivors to their fate. The men were rescued a few hours later by the Mexican tanker *Fajo de Oro*.

On preliminary dives I noticed that the wreck listed to starboard rather than to port. I shrugged it off as one of those vagaries of sinking in turbulent seas. After several exploratory dives, I had what one might consider the experience of a lifetime – if I had not already had a number of exhilarating experiences in other aspects of life. My buddy was Lois Impagliazo. We descended the anchor line to 155 feet, then swam toward an area that

Dennis Clark took this snapshot of the final moments of the *Manuela*. He was a crewmember aboard the *Norwich City*.

I had previously determined, by the presence of a stainless steel electric range, to be the galley. We were scrounging in the muck for china dishes (of which we recovered several), when a dark gray shadow loomed menacingly overhead.

Although sand tiger sharks are not known to be overly aggressive, all sharks are unpredictable. I took the opportunity to photograph one from underneath, in order to capture its snaggle-toothed appearance. Another shark meandered by a moment later. I snapped the shutter again. The strobe illuminated the broad girth of the white belly. Then another shark appeared – and yet another. They ranged in length from five to seven feet. Each cruised slowly, almost lazily, casting dark and ominous glances in our direction. Soon, Lois and I were looking up at a phalanx of sand tigers. They swarmed over the wreckage about eight feet above the bottom, rippling collectively like a canvas tarp in a gentle but silent breeze.

Lois clung to me like a limpet. She wasn't terrified, but she was justifiably watchful – and perhaps a trifle nervous. Together we confronted the oncoming horde. Two divers wearing double tanks and blowing noisy exhaust bubbles presented a more aggressive posture to curious predators than two single divers on the flee.

I ascended into the solid stream of sharks. Blunt snouts veered left and right, avoiding collision with the raucous wetsuited stranger of equivalent size. I wanted close-ups. I held the detached strobe to the side as a particularly toothsome monster approached obliquely. I tripped the shutter as it passed within a couple of feet of my camera. The flash elicited no response. The creature moseyed along. I heard the whine of the recharging capacitor.

An abrupt flurry of activity commenced to my left. An adjacent shark bent double in the middle of its long, lank body, lunged sideways, and wrapped its mouth around the strobe in front of my face. Powerful jaws clamped jagged teeth around the flashtube assembly. A cloud of filth erupted. I reacted instinctively. Thinking that the shark had just crushed and flooded my expensive strobe, in one smooth motion I let the camera rig drop to the end of its wrist lanyard, and threw an angry

overhand punch with my right fist. I was aiming for the gill slits, but the shark moved away so fast that I caught it farther back along the side, burying my fist in the soft flesh halfway to the wrist. The shark took off like a runaway missile, its body gyrating wildly, and disappeared among the mass of moving brethren. I had just proved that I was bigger and badder than it was.

I descended below the layer of sharks. A hasty examination of the strobe revealed two rows of teeth marks: one across the lens and one along the top of the housing. But the watertight integrity appeared to be intact. The cloud of filth must have been regurgitated food instead of short-circuiting electronic components. Sharks are sensitive to electricity. They are stimulated to aggressive behavior by fluctuating currents. The shark had not attacked me, but the recycling capacitor. I was not mollified by this intellectual concession.

Lois yanked my arm. She pointed in the direction of the anchor line. But I had one more job to do. I secured a liftbag to the stainless steel range, added air from my mouthpiece to the liftbag, and sent the range through the ceiling of sharks. Several sand tigers followed the liftbag to the surface, which the exceptional visibility permitted us to see. Lois and I made good our escape. I wondered what she was thinking during our long decompression.

Another dive on the *Malchace* provided excitement of a different variety. While exploring the bow I spotted a thin curved bronze lip protruding from the seabed. My heart thumped in anticipation as I dug sand out of the bowl of what could have been a steam valve.

When I felt the clapper, I knew that I had found the ship's bell.

I could not free the bell because it was still secured to its davit, which was buried – and which was apparently bolted to a section of steel decking. The ultimate recovery required several more dives and a great deal of help from a number of people. After excavating the bell, I attached a liftbag and secured the anchor line to a series of three C-clamps that I had fastened to the bell. The skipper backed the boat until the tension ripped the bell and davit free. The already inflated liftbag then floated the bell to the surface unattended.

A few minutes of chipping revealed the name stamped in bronze: *Manuela*. The *Manuela* was torpedoed by the *U-404*, with the loss of three lives. The men of the merchant marine took a savage beating at the hands – and the torpedoes – of German U-boats. Their sacrifice has gone largely unacknowledged.

The *Manuela* had been misidentified in the 1943 wreck survey that was conducted by the Coast Guard cutter *Gentian*. The mistake implied that the wreck, noted on the chart as the *Manuela,* was instead the *Malchace*. My later observations of the other wreck – which lay a mile away at 205 feet – confirmed it.

The reversal of names now stands corrected.

Shuffled Shipwrecks of North Carolina

Part 1

Two shipwrecks are identified on the charts as the *Buarque* and the *Equipoise.* German U-boats sank both of them during World War Two, off the coast of North Carolina close to the border of Virginia. The way they are listed, the *Buarque* lies inshore at a depth of 140 feet. The *Equipoise* lies offshore at a depth of 250 feet.

The *Gentian* surveyed the offshore site in 1944. According to the report, "A study of the underwater photographs and other information available relative to the wreck does not shed any light on its identity. Its designation on the wreck list has therefore been changed from 'Probably *Equipoise*' to 'Probably *Buarque.*' " Despite this admonition, neither the chart nor the wreck list was changed, and the offshore site retained the name of *Equipoise.* The inshore site was therefore called the *Buarque.* And so it remained throughout the years as head boats fished the wrecks.

No one had ever dived on the offshore wreck until July 3, 1992. That was when Mike Boring, skipper of the *Sea Hunter*, took six divers to explore the site. These divers were Ken Clayton, Peter Feuerle, Steve Gatto, Jon Hulburt, Tom Packer, and this author.

I recovered a pair of gauges that confirmed the *Gentian's* deduction that the offshore wreck was the *Buarque.* The gauges were manufactured by the Moeller Instrument Company of Brooklyn, New York, and were stamped "Made in U.S.A." The *Buarque* was built at Hog Island, Pennsylvania, whereas the *Equipoise* was built at Glasgow, Scotland.

Ergo, the inshore wreck must be the *Equipoise.* Or

so I inferred. I had already corrected another reversal of names that the charts and the *Gentian* had made. When I recovered a bell from a wreck that was supposed to be the *Malchace*, I found that the name stamped in bronze was *Manuela*. I later identified the other wreck – which lay only a mile away – as the *Malchace*.

Due to its shallow depth, the inshore wreck, which I now presumed was the *Equipoise*, was a popular dive site. I first dived it on October 4, 1993. I conducted my standard survey, made a detailed drawing of the layout, and noted particular features.

On another trip two years later, Jeff Hewlett apprised me of his observations of the so-called *Equipoise*. He, too, had made a detailed drawing of the wreck, but he went one step further: he and a group of friends measured the length with a tape measure. Although the bow was broken off, making a precise measurement difficult to obtain, he calculated that the total length was 270 feet. The length of the *Equipoise* was 429 feet. Even allowing for imprecision, he could not have made a mistake of 159 feet.

Jeff and his friends also measured the beam. There was some slight sagging of the hull plates in places, but by measuring a number of areas they obtained a beam of 38 to 40 feet. The beam of the *Equipoise* was 54 feet.

He submitted that the wreck could not possibly be the *Equipoise*. It took me no longer than a couple of seconds to mull this over and agree with him. I knew that he was on to something, for as I pictured the wreck in my mind, I realized that I had not swum 429 feet from bow to stern.

Jeff's argument raised two immediate questions: what wreck was it, and where was the *Equipoise*?

We had no working hypothesis other than the fact that the inshore wreck had likely *not* been built in the U.S. This interpretation was predicated upon the helm stand that Hal and Penny Good had recovered from the wheelhouse area. The top of the stand was stamped "The Pepper Steering Gear," "R. Roger & Co.," and

Buarque. (Official U.S. Coast Guard photo.)

"Stockton-on-Tees." Originally, these stampings lent credence to the theory that the wreck was the *Equipoise.* What they meant now was anyone's guess.

I recovered an old-style taffrail log that was no longer in use by World War Two. Modern logs consisted of two parts: a register that was secured to the rail, and a rotator that was suspended in the water astern of the vessel. My log was a self-contained type, in which the rotator was connected by means of a shaft to geared clocklike faces in the main body of the log; the entire assembly was submerged. I inferred from this log that the wreck must be old, possibly predating World War One.

At home, I scanned the wreck lists that I had collected during more than two decades of research. I found nothing in the area that conformed to the inshore wreck. I started asking people who had dived on the wreck if they knew of any other recoveries that might indicate a name or place of origin. Gene Peterson provided a clue that proved to be crucial. He told me that he found the hub of the auxiliary steering wheel; the wooden spokes had been eaten away. On his next dive, he took Rich Allen to the stern, and together they recovered the spokeless hub. On the face of the hub was stamped MEXICANO. Gene thought it was the place of construction: Mexico. To me it sounded like a manufacturer's name.

Nonetheless, in my personal library I looked up *Mexicano* in the shipwreck researcher's bible, *Encyclopedia of American Shipwrecks.* No *Mexicano* was listed. However, I found a *Mexicano* listed in *Dictionary of Disasters at Sea During the Age of Steam 1824-1962.*

According to the entry, a British tanker by the name of *Mexicano* foundered on September 17, 1903, during a voyage from Philadelphia to Vera Cruz. No location was given. A voyage from Philadelphia to Mexico implied a coastal route.

Armed with this information, I went to the Independence Seaport Museum to look through maritime newspapers. According to the *Lloyd's Weekly Shipping Index*, the *Mexicano* foundered in rough seas when "a wave crashed through the deck and flooded the fire-room, rendering the steamer helpless." The British steamer *Roxby* rescued a sailor named Reyarberay, who was clinging to some wreckage. He thought he was the sole survivor. Then the steamship *Vidar* was reported to have found six more survivors "clinging to pieces of wreckage." No location was given.

Next I tried the *New York Maritime Register*. The account was similar, but added this important tidbit: the *Mexicano* "foundered off the Florida coast night of Sep 15 during a hurricane."

Dead end. I was looking for a *Mexicano* that sank 500 miles north of the Florida-Georgia border.

As usual, I made photocopies of all the reference materials and stuffed them into a file folder that I created for the project. Just to be thorough, I looked up *Mexicano* in the *Lloyd's Register*, in order to ascertain if there were any other vessels of the same name in the same time period. There was only one: a tanker. I photocopied the page anyway.

Soon afterward, Jeff sent me copies of his survey drawings. As I filed them, I decided to review the maritime newspaper articles. Now I saw something that I had missed before, and that was contradictory.

Equipoise. (Courtesy of the National Archives.)

Although the *Mexicano* supposedly foundered off the coast of Florida, an appended item farther down the page mentioned that the *Vidar* picked up the six men "in lat 36 16, lon 75 55." That latitude was nowhere near Florida. I pulled out my nautical charts and, with a pair of dividers, pinpointed the position of the rescue. Lo and behold, the men were picked up only five miles from site of the inshore wreck.

That was too much for coincidence! The statement about Florida had to be erroneous.

I looked at the *Mexicano's* statistics. She was built in 1893 in Sunderland, England. She was powered by a triple expansion reciprocating steam engine. She measured 270 feet in length, and 38 feet abeam: the exact dimensions that Jeff had measured with his tape.

Voila!

I immediately wrote to Jeff to give him the news.

Contemporary newspaper articles furnished the human drama. According to August Osterlind, "About 4 o'clock on Sept. 15 we encountered a severe hurricane, blowing from the south. About 12 o'clock it shifted to northwest and blew with tremendous force. A heavy sea swept the steamer from stem to stern, carrying away the lifeboats and ventilators, flooding the engine rooms, and putting out the fires. The steamer then became unmanageable and was soon in the trough of the sea.

"She rolled about for a little over an hour, when she sank stern first. The men in the forecastle were called out and told to be ready to save themselves the best way possible when the steamer went down. The boatswain refused to leave his bunk, saying if he had to die he would rather die in his bunk than in the sea. Two firemen refused to leave the stokeroom, preferring to take a chance on the steamer standing out the storm.

"We were on the bridge with the officers and jumped overboard just as the steamer went down. Just before I jumped I heard two pistol shots, and I think some of the officers shot themselves, preferring that kind of death to drowning.

"We drifted about for several hours, doing our best to keep together, but when daylight came there were but seven of us together. The second mate was exhausted. He took off his lifebuoy, handed it to one of the sailors, said good-bye to all of us, and went down. We had about given up hope when we sighted the steamer."

Aboard the *Vidar*, Captain Sorrensen was sitting in his cabin when "I heard a cry. Thinking some one was fooling on board the steamer, I went out on the bridge to investigate. When I reached the bridge I heard the cry again. The sound seemed to come from the ocean, but I could not see any one.

"I ordered a boat to be gotten ready, and when I heard the cry a third time I saw something in the water like a small log, about half a mile off. With the aid of my glass I found it to be a small hatch, with a man in oil-skins stretched full length on it.

"I immediately steered for the man and rescued him; he was completely exhausted, and had to be hauled aboard the boat. He was unable to say a word, and thinking there were no more, as I could see no wreckage about, I started on my way.

"I had proceeded about a mile when I saw several objects in the water which I could not plainly make out. Upon going closer I found five more men clinging to pieces of wreckage. I had the boat lowered again and picked up the castaways. They, too, were exhausted, and one was nearly crazy. My men had to hold him in the lifeboat, for he was determined to jump into the sea.

"There was another steamer some distance off and I could see that they had a lifeboat out, but I could not distinguish her name."

Captain Shields, master of the *Roxby*, organized the rescue of Domingo Ballo Reyarberay. According to the lone survivor's account, he "went under with the vessel, and by merest chance became entangled in some loose rigging and spars. The buoyancy of these brought him to the surface, and he made himself fast to the larger spar. For seven hours he floated in a turbulent sea, until finally the *Roxby* hove in sight."

Captain King and fourteen men went to a watery grave.

By means of exploration and archival research, a mystery was solved and a dramatic tale of survival was brought to light.

What about the *Equipoise*? To this day, nobody knows the wreck's whereabouts.

Part 2

In the 1970's, when I began conducting historical research for my Popular Dive Guide Series, I noticed certain aberrations with respect to the location and identification of World War Two shipwrecks.

One prime example is the *Cayru.* This large passenger-freighter was torpedoed by a German U-boat off the coast of New Jersey. Wartime Naval documents provided coordinates of the site. In 1950, the U.S. Coast and Geodetic Survey conducted a wire-drag survey of the wreck, and subsequently plotted its position on the charts. Despite this apparent authentication, no one has ever been able to locate the wreck.

I organized several search trips that came to naught. I also continued my archival research. Eventually I unearthed the original Descriptive Report of the 1950 survey. I was shocked to learn that the surveyors stated specifically that they had *not* located the wreck, and in fact recommended that the wreck symbol be deleted from the chart. For some reason, the symbol was never deleted, and still appears today on modern charts.

San Delfino's sister, *San Cirilo.* (Courtesy of the Steamship Historical Society of America.)

The *Cayru* has yet to be found. Probably it lies far offshore. Corroboration for this likelihood can be found in the deck log of the *U-94*, in which Oberleutnant zur See Otto Ites recorded coordinates that are farther off the coast than Allied documents indicate.

This was my introduction to the fact that neither the historical records nor the nautical charts were gospel. From that point onward I harbored suspicions.

I passed these suspicions on to my readers and fellow researchers whenever possible. In my 1993 publication of *Shipwrecks of North Carolina: from the Diamond Shoals North*, I posted a warning about the identification of the *San Delfino*. After this tanker was torpedoed by a German U-boat, she was "last seen afire from stem to stern, but afloat." No onc actually witnessed the sinking of the vessel.

In 1943 and 1944, the U.S. Coast Guard cutter *Gentian* conducted underwater surveys off the eastern seaboard, the purpose of which was to locate and identify the sunken fleet of U-boat casualties. Once a wreck was located, geologists from the Lamont Doherty Institute lowered a watertight drop camera to the bottom, and snapped pictures of the hull and superstructure.

One such photograph provided positive proof of the wreck's identity: captured on film were the bronze letters on the bow. They spelled COIMBRA. Other identifications were more tentative, even speculative. In fact, the *Gentian* misnamed a number of shipwrecks. Perhaps she even misidentified more wrecks than she properly identified.

One wreck that she identified as the *Ario* turned out to be the *Bedfordshire*. The *Gentian* then claimed to have located the *Ario* in a different location, but when Navy divers recovered the bell in 1944, that wreck proved to be the *Dixie Arrow*.

The *Ario* was ever elusive. . . .

On August 7, 1944, the *Gentian* surveyed a wreck that stood "80' high in 187' of water" east of Oregon Inlet, North Carolina. According to the survey report, a search of the records revealed "no previously reported positions of wrecks lie within many miles of this position, nor had any instrument contacts been obtained by ASW vessels operating in the area." Also, "only one vessel whose wreck cannot be located with reasonable certainty was sunk near this position. This is the . . . British tanker *San Delfino*."

The report noted, "The unburned lines and wooden planking would seem to make it unlikely that this is the wreck of the *San Delfino*." Nonetheless, a wreck symbol was placed on the chart, and it was annotated as the *San Delfino*.

In the chapter on the *Ciltvaira* in the same book, I noted these incongruities as well as the saga of the *Ciltvaira's* two-day drift. The wreck that local anglers and divers called the *Ciltvaira* lay only a few miles from shore. Yet the *Ciltvaira* was torpedoed 35 miles northeast of Cape Hatteras, and was seen to be drifting northward. In my mind, these items of information cast great doubt on the identifications of these two wrecks. Lacking any firm proof, I proposed that the wreck known locally as the *Ciltvaira* (alias the Green Buoy Wreck) might be the *Mirlo*: a tanker that was torpedoed close to shore in World War One, and whose remains had never been identified. Based on the evidence that I had at the time, that was my best hypothesis.

I wrote, "It is possible that the wreck only tentatively identified by the *Gentian* as the *San Delfino* could prove to be the *Ciltvaira*. An open mind, a diligent search, and direct observation of that wreck or newly-acquired hang numbers will someday lead to its discovery." These prophetic words later bore fruit, but not the kind of fruit that I had envisioned.

It was good that I noted the inconclusive evidence of the naming of these wrecks, for my written suspicions alerted the wreck-diving community not to take any of the World War Two identifications for granted.

The first person to take my admonitions seriously was Robert Smith. In 1996, he wrote to me about his speculation that the names of the *Papoose* and *W.E. Hutton* were reversed. What made this scenario attrac-

Ciltvaira under tow. Note the lack of a deck gun. (Courtesy of the National Archives.)

tive were the similarities between the two vessels: both were tankers, their dimensions were nearly the same, each was propelled by a triple expansion reciprocating steam engine, each consumed diesel for fuel, they were built one year apart, and - coincidental but irrelevant - both were constructed in California (but by different shipbuilders).

Smith asked for my assistance. I reviewed my files, but found nothing conclusive in my records that could either affirm or negate his speculation. The only help that I could offer was advice: recover some artifact that could be attributed to only one of the vessels. Smith and his cohorts worked assiduously in this vein for years, but were unable to find a smoking gun that pointed at either vessel. Yet their work did not go unnoticed. While some may have thought that Smith and his associates were barking up the wrong tree, other wreck-divers were recovering artifacts from different World War Two wrecks: artifacts that eventually led to sorting out the shuffled shipwrecks, albeit in unanticipated identifications.

By 2000, however, Smith had uncovered an important item of information. He learned that Johann Mohr, skipper of the *U-124*, claimed that the *W.E. Hutton* sank at a depth of 100 to 130 feet. The wreck that was being called the *W.E. Hutton* lay in 70 feet of water. This led Smith to speculate that perhaps this shallow-water wreck was instead the *Ario*, the tanker that had never been found (or identified). The *Ario* was identical to the *W.E. Hutton* with regard to tonnage, dimensions, and propulsion unit, and was constructed in the same year by the same shipbuilder (although at different yards). They were essentially sister ships whose resemblance was not to be taken lightly.

One definite but minor difference between them was the number of masts: two on the *W.E. Hutton*, three on the *Ario*. After decades of collapse, these features could not be observed on the wrecks. There was also a slight difference in the forecastle construction, but again this was not discernible under water.

Several years later, Smith informed me that his friend Dale Hansen proved conclusively that the wreck that was called the *W.E. Hutton* was indeed the *Ario*, and that the wreck that was called the *Papoose* was instead the *W.E. Hutton*.

According to this scenario, the *Papoose* was the wreck that had never been found, and with good reason. Her sinking was not actually observed. She was last seen drifting northward.

In addition to Hansen's exhaustive research, the new evidence that led to this conclusion was the observation of battle damage. Perhaps even more telling was the recovery of a plaque with the name Socony-Vacuum stamped in bronze. Socony-Vacuum owned the *Ario* at the time of her loss. The Pure Oil Company owned the *W.E. Hutton*.

Elsewhere, in 1993, Roger Hunting recovered the aiming mechanism from the deck gun of the wreck that was called the *Ciltvaira*, but which I had proved conclusively in the 1980's could not possibly be the *Ciltvaira*. Aerial photographs of the *Ciltvaira*, low in the water

Ario. (Official U.S. Coast Guard photo.)

after being torpedoed, clearly show that she was not equipped with a deck gun; archival records corroborated that she was unarmed. Because the *Mirlo* was armed, and was lost in the vicinity of the wreck that was called the *Ciltvaira*, I had considered the possibility that – as noted above – the wreck might be the *Mirlo*.

The aiming mechanism had two disks: one for vertical positioning and one for horizontal positioning. The horizontal positioning disk was stamped 1917. The vertical positioning disk was reversible, depending upon the muzzle velocity of the charge. One side of the vertical positioning disk was stamped 1918; the other side was stamped 1940.

When Hunting told me this, I hoped (or prayed) that "1940" was a serial number, or a part number. But when he showed me the disk in person, there was little doubt in my mind that it looked like a date. This threw me into a quandary. I conceded that the wreck could not be the *Mirlo*, and must therefore be a World War Two wreck. But what wreck was it? And where was the *Mirlo*?

Elsewhere, also in 1993, Greg Masi recovered a helm from the wreck that was called the *San Delfino*. This helm was made by the Standard Brass and Manufacturing Company, in Port Arthur, Texas. What was an American-made helm doing on a tanker that was supposedly built in England?

Then, in June 1994, Ted Green recovered a shell casing from the wreck that was called the *Ciltvaira*. Stamped on the brass base were the British broad

W.E. Hutton. (Official U.S. Coast Guard photo.)

Papoose. (Official U.S. Coast Guard photo.)

arrow and the date of manufacture: 1940. He and I pondered this new evidence at the time. I considered the far-out possibility that the shell was from a British armed trawler (a number of which had been assigned to operate as escorts in American waters) - perhaps fired coincidentally over the wreck site. The expended shell was then ejected overboard. But I didn't really believe it. The shell casing was yet another piece of evidence against the wreck being the *Mirlo*.

In 1997, Gene Peterson recovered the hydraulic steering telemotor from the alleged *San Delfino*. Stamped on the hub of the helm was "MACTAGGART-SCOTT & CO. LTD EDINBURG." A plaque provided the patent number and a serial number. This was consistent with the fact that the *San Delfino* was constructed in England, adjacent to Scottish suppliers in Edinburgh.

Peterson's artifact seemed to confirm the wreck's identity as the *San Delfino*, while Masi's artifact seemed to contradict it. The plot thickened.

The puzzle pieces began to fit together in 2006. Until that time, the wreck that was known as the *Ciltvaira*, or the Green Buoy Wreck, had a nearly intact hull. By now the plates were peeling off so that the machinery spaces were exposed. This enabled Uwe Lovas to observe that the propulsion unit consisted of a pair of inline diesel engines that drove a single propeller.

Mike Barnette delved into these matters with some

insightful historical research. The passages in my North Carolina book, regarding the *Gentian* survey and the doubt about the identity of the so-called *San Delfino*, now assumed primary importance. As also noted in my book, the *Papoose* was a phoenix that had arisen from the ashes of the *Silvanus*, which was destroyed by fire on the Mississippi River after colliding with the *Thomas M. Wheeler*, in 1926.

The MacTaggart Scott Company was still in business. Barnette sent them an e-mail with the serial number from Peterson's helm. Company records confirmed that the helm was sold for installation on the *Silvanus*, which was being reconstructed and which was renamed *Papoose*. This was positive proof that the wreck that was called the *San Delfino* was in fact the *Papoose* at the end of her long drift.

This meant that the *San Delfino* was now among the missing, misidentified, or unidentified wrecks. Circumstantial evidence led Barnette to conclude that the wreck that was called the *Ciltvaira*, or the Green Buoy Wreck, was in reality the *San Delfino*.

As noted above, the *Ciltvaira* was unarmed, and the date on Hunting's disk precluded the wreck from being the *Mirlo*. More compelling than this negative evidence is the fact that the *San Delfino* was propelled by twin diesel engines: a rarity among propulsion units.

The way the identities stand now, the so-called *Papoose* is the *W.E. Hutton*; the so-called *W.E. Hutton* is the *Ario*; the so-called *San Delfino* is the *Papoose*; and the so-called *Ciltvaira* is the *San Delfino*. According to this new scenario, the *Ciltvaira* is the missing wreck, and the *Mirlo* has never been found.

The end
Or is it?

Gold from the Ella Warley

Often I have found shipwreck information by means of serendipity: while researching one wreck, I have accidentally uncovered documents pertaining to another wreck that I was not consciously researching, or to a wreck that I wrote about years ago, or to a wreck that is on my list of future research projects.

For example, after publication of *Shipwrecks of New Jersey: North*, I stumbled upon additional information about the *Ella Warley*: not about her loss but about the lawsuit that resulted from it. The *Ella Warley* was a sidewheel steamer that sank in 1863 as a result of collision with the SS *North Star*.

According to certain court documents, "The suit was tried upon libel and cross libel, both vessels found in fault, and the damages ordered to be divided."

Attorneys for the *Ella Warley* appealed the court's decision, citing the liability limitation law. This law constitutes one of the most absurd concepts ever conceived in jurisprudence. It stipulates that the financial liability of a vessel's owner is limited to the value of said vessel after collision. A million-dollar vessel that suffered two hundred thousand dollars in damage (the cost of repairs), and was consequently valued at eight hundred thousand dollars, limited the owner's liability to that amount – even if the other vessel constituted a total loss of many millions of dollars.

Imagine the hoopla such a law would create if it pertained to automobile collisions. Any owner found liable would not have to pay any claims that exceeded the value of his vehicle after the collision. In other words, the liable owner of a thousand-dollar junker that suffered only minor damage, might have to pay the owner of a Cadillac – which was totally demolished – no more than a few dollars in restitution! Go figure.

Extrapolating from this scenario, if the liable owner's car was totaled, he would escape scot-free from all resulting claims: for injuries, for fatalities, and for damage to other vehicles and to any other property – even if the driver was inebriated at the time of the so-called "accident."

This absurdity of maritime law is always invoked in order to protect the liable owner from paying his just due. It may come as no surprise that most of the Congressional representatives who framed this law and voted for its passage were major stockholders in shipping companies.

Be that as it may, the value of the *Ella Warley* at the bottom of the sea was essentially zero. Her owner's attorneys argued that her owner was therefore not responsible for paying his half of the loss. This absurdity was compounded when the attorneys argued that the owners of the *North Star* should pay the owners of the *Ella Warley* for their half of the loss: a clear case of eating their cake and having it too.

The court disagreed with this tautological unreasoning. "According to the general maritime law, in cases of collision occurring by the fault of both parties, the entire damage to both ships is added together in one common mass, and equally divided between them, and thereupon arises a liability of one party to pay the other such sum as is necessary to equalize the burden. This is the rule of mutual liability between the parties."

And so the case ended.

At the time of publication (2000), I had not encountered anyone who had even heard the name of the ship, much less anyone who knew the location of the wreck. I noted this observation at the end of the chapter.

Lo and behold, several months after publication, I received correspondence from Florida, from one Allan Gardner. He used to live in New Jersey. In 1976, Gardner "worked" the wreck of a sidewheel steamer with his friend Paul Hepler. They "worked" the wreck because two gold coins had been recovered recently from the site. Inspired by these accidental finds, Gardner and Hepler built an airlift to move enormous quantities of sand from the buried wooden hull.

They found no gold coins, but Gardner did recover the handle of a spoon on which was engraved the last part of a name: "LEY". He looked through a book that contained a list of vessel losses, and found the name *Ella Warley*, which went down precisely where the wreck was located (and which I specified in my book).

Gardner then ascertained the circumstances of the vessel's loss from contemporary newspaper accounts. Because the wreck was supposed to have gone down with $8,000 in gold, and an iron safe containing $5,000 in an unspecified form, he and Hepler kept their "work" a closely guarded secret.

Despite their lack of success with the airlift, Gardner and Hepler returned to the wreck the following year: this time looking only for lobsters. Hepler went down first. He came back to the boat with a handful of gold coins that he found without even digging – they were lying on top of the sand! Undoubtedly, the sand had been shifted by hurricanes or winter storms. Gardner went down next, and found more gold coins in the same spot: American gold pieces in denominations of $5, $10, and $20.

Gardner and Hepler maintained their secret throughout the years – until Gardner fortuitously read about the *Ella Warley* in my book. When I contacted Gardner and asked for the full particulars of the story, in order to give him and Hepler credit in the next edition of the book, he provided the information that I have written above. Thus another item of interest has been added to the history of the *Ella Warley*.

China Wreck Candidates

John Sidney and Medway

This piece is about the China Wreck: an unidentified sailing vessel that sank in 45 feet of water off the coast of Delaware. The wooden hull is packed with British china, hence the name. Research of recovered items indicates that the dates of manufacture of this china are probably between 1869 and 1873.

In *Shipwrecks of Delaware and Maryland* (2002), I detailed Joan Charles's justification for identifying the wreck as the *D.H. Bills*, which disappeared with all hands in 1880, while transporting 37 tons of earthenware from England to Wilmington, North Carolina. A tremendous storm that struck the U.S. eastern seaboard coincided with the vessel's estimated time of arrival. Charles hopefully presumed that the *D.H. Bills* was carrying old china that had been kept in storage for a number of years – old or outdated stock that we might call "remainders" today.

Charles was cautious. Instead of claiming categorically that the *D.H. Bills* was the China Wreck, she stated only that the vessel was a good "candidate." Another candidate that she originally considered was the *John Sidney*. However, she eventually disqualified the *John Sidney* because, according to her research, that vessel sank in 1870 – effectively predating the dates of manufacture of some of the china.

Research is sometimes serendipitous. For example, while researching shipwrecks of Massachusetts, I happened upon a newspaper article from October 30, 1872, which mentioned the loss of the sailing vessel *John Sidney*. My mind is a storehouse of shipwreck names. The name jumped out at me. I don't always remember the circumstances that surround a familiar name; sometimes I cannot even place the name in geographical context. I just *know* that it *is* a shipwreck. In such cases, I *always* copy the information, then check my files at home.

In this case, however, I had no difficulty in making the association, for the article specifically stated that the *John Sidney* "struck on October 24 on McCrie's Shoal, 12 miles from Cape Henlopen, during a gale, and filled. The crew were saved and landed at Lewes, Del. The vessel and cargo will be a total loss, as she was breaking up on the 25th and the cargo floating away. Some 36 bbls [barrels] whiskey washed ashore, and were secured." She was bound from Liverpool to Philadelphia, under the command of Captain Bartlett. The vessel was listed as a steamer that grossed 1,002 tons; her port of registry was Richmond, Maine.

The newspaper also noted the loss of another vessel in the same gale, on nearby Hen and Chickens Shoal (farther south and close to the beach). She was the bark *Medway*, from London. She was lost on the "night of Oct 25th." Also lost at the same time and in the same gale was the bark *Liepabakarka*. She ran aground on Cape May, New Jersey, while transporting a cargo of coffee from Rio de Janeiro to New York.

These nuggets of information comprised the tip of an informational iceberg that was buried in other repositories (some of which were located within my own

Maker's marks on the reverse side of the china plates.

library). Once again I resumed research on the China Wreck.

From other sources, I corroborated the correct date of the loss of the *John Sidney*: October 24, 1872. She was carrying iron and "general merchandise." I also ascertained from registry records that she was *not* a steamer, but a full-rigged ship. (This lends credence to the old motto: don't believe everything that you read in the newspapers.) She measured 169 feet in length. The *Medway* measured 129 feet in length.

Other sources verified the circumstances of these losses, and provided additional information. All twenty-four members of the *John Sidney* rowed ashore safely in lifeboats. The *Medway's* crew were not so fortunate: four men perished when their lifeboat overturned, while "the Captain and part of the crew landed safely" at Lewes. "Two of the missing crew were picked up by a pilot-boat. One dead body was found in the boat."

What does this new information lead me to conclude? Could the China Wreck be the remains of either the *John Sidney* or the *Medway*?

Both vessels had metalled hulls. This means that the wooden hull was strengthened by means of iron straps. This fact is consistent with iron strapping found on the wreck site.

The *John Sidney* stranded on McCrie's Shoal, which is two to three miles northeast of the wreck site. The *Medway* ran aground on Hen and Chickens Shoal,

Maker's marks on the reverse side of the china plates.

Some china plates were painted on the obverse side. Because the pictures in the bowl were surrounded by the letters of the alphabet, these plates are called ABC plates.

which is eight miles southwest. Sources indicate that both wrecks "broke up" or "went to pieces." These descriptions imply that either hull could have drifted or been driven to where the China Wreck lies today.

The wreck site is located fairly close to where the *John Sidney* stranded, and in a direction in which the vessel would have drifted or been driven. However, the wreck measures approximately 125 feet in length, far short of the length of the *John Sidney* – unless the vessel broke in two, and the missing section disintegrated or remains buried under the shoal.

The length of the *Medway* is almost identical to the measured length of the China Wreck. However, it is unlikely that the *Medway* would have drifted in a northeast direction, and for such a distance.

Both wrecks are contenders, with the *John Sidney* having my personal vote between the two. A cargo manifest would be helpful.

By the way, some of the floating barrels of whiskey that were "secured" were actually "imbibed."

I was such an active diver in the 1970's that I belonged to as many as five dive clubs, and dived with a number of others when space was available. One purpose of a dive club was to organize dive trips and boat charters for its members. Another was to introduce newly certified and novice divers to the underwater realm.

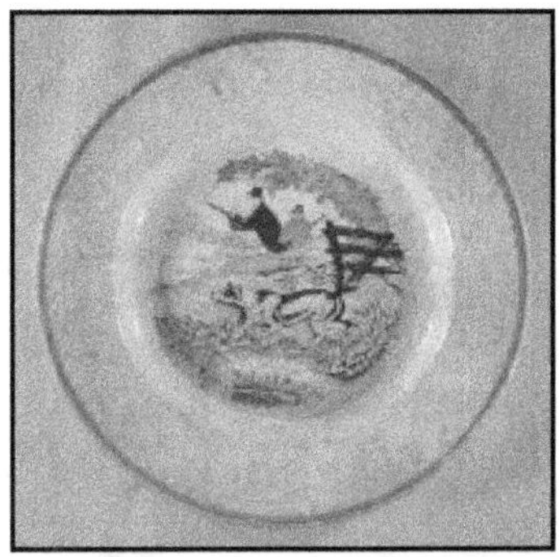

Divers have found ABC plates in a multitude of designs. These plates are highly sought by collectors. Similar plates can be found in antique shops. They command a high price.

One such introductory dive took place on June 13, 1976. I escorted George Hughes down the anchor line and around the China Wreck. He dived with a single tank; I dived with doubles. We explored the wreck together. I pointed out stacks of china that were encrusted together in the hull. I broke some plates free and placed them in my mesh bag.

When his tank got low on air, I took him back to the grapnel and signaled for him to return to the boat on his own. I continued my dive. I spent a total of 100 minutes on the bottom, at a depth of 45 feet. According to the Navy Tables that I used at the time, a short decompression was required. I did my hang, then surfaced - the last person to return to the boat.

My fellow club members duly informed me that I was the first person in history to make a decompression dive on the China Wreck.

George Hughes went on to become a skilled and dedicated diver.

Megalodon
Fossil Shark Teeth

This chapter takes a different tack from my usual fare about shipwrecks.

Let's go back a bit to my teenage years. I have had a strong and abiding interest in fossils. One of my prize possessions is *The Fossil Book*, by Carroll Lane Fenton. I asked for it for Christmas when I was fifteen years old. Naturally, I still have it – along with the other 9,000 books that I've read since then. I never throw away a book that I've read. Although my personal collection rivals the inventory of many public libraries (and is causing my house to settle more than my neighbor's), I take great pleasure in being able to refer to books that have been such an important and fulfilling part of my life.

My collection consists of more than one hundred books on paleontology, geology, and archaeology (as well as many hundreds of books on other scientific subjects). In college I took courses in all three disciplines. My primary goal was to become a paleontologist. Then came the Vietnam war. I got drafted between semesters. Afterward, I had to work for a living, so my college education foundered. But I maintained my interest in fossils throughout my life.

That's why a trip to the Cooper River in South Carolina to dive for fossil shark teeth meant so much to me. I went in the winter when the temperature was too cold for most wetsuit divers. I was comfortable in my drysuit. Visibility was one to two feet. Once slack tide passed, I found it nearly impossible to stop from being swept downstream with the raging current. But I stuck it out. During the course of a weekend I recovered more than a dozen fine specimens from the riverbed. They ranged in size from one to three inches.

Although the Cooper River is considered a hotbed for fossil shark teeth, I have recently been introduced to a more productive location: an ancient river delta off the coast of South Carolina. Rob Penn discovered this area several years ago. He was spearfishing on an off-shore ledge that was a prehistoric coastline during the Ice Age, when so much water was bound in glacial ice that the shore extended more than forty miles east of its present position.

A woman on his boat recovered a curious triangular-shaped rock. She showed it to Rob, who immediately recognized it as a tooth. And not just any tooth, but the tooth of a *Carcharodon megalodon.*

Megalodon sharks – the biggest sharks that ever lived – roamed those ancient seas for millions of years: from fifty million years ago to a couple of million years ago. Their fifty-foot-long skeletons were cartilaginous instead of bony, and were too soft to remain intact to become fossilized; they quickly dissolved into their component chemicals. Their teeth were dispersed by currents and tides, but were hard enough to survive the millennia.

This is my haul from my second dive on what Rob Penn affectionately calls the "boneyard." Some people clean off the encrustation with vinegar, but I like to leave it in place so the teeth look like they came from under the sea. A simple freshwater bath will remove ionic mineral deposits. If the teeth are allowed to dry without freshwater treatment, they may crack as the sodium and chlorine crystallize to form sodium chloride - salt - an effect that is similar to frost heaves in road surfaces.

Here is a collection of fossilized whale bones from my second dive in the offshore boneyard. The round bone in the upper left is a vertebra. The others are ribs.

A tooth consists of three major parts: pulp, dentin, and enamel. The soft pulp covers chambers and root canals in the jaw. It is surrounded by a hard material called dentin, which is calcareous (containing calcium). Dentin is coated with enamel that protects the interior parts from the constant grind of chewing.

These megalodon teeth practically carpeted the primeval riverbed that is now the distant seabed. Rob found the greatest concentration of meg teeth among coral heads on ledges that were formed when long-ago waves washed away the banks of an ancient water-course. And that was where he took me, on his boat that he appropriately named the *Play Penn*.

It wasn't the greatest day to be at sea aboard a 25-foot center console boat, with no protection from the sun, wind, and spray. It was crowded with six people, tanks, and dive gear. But hey – we were guaranteed shark teeth.

Rob – the original offshore megalodontist – anchored the boat and dived alone to 100 feet to find a productive area, leaving his ten-year-old son Kyle to work as topside crew. Rob returned with a couple of fine specimens. Then the first team descended. Mike Moore and Chris Campbell also surfaced with fine specimens. Then it was my turn. My buddy was my long-time soul mate, Pete Manchee.

My first dive was almost disappointing. I was thirty-four minutes into digging through gravel before I found my first tooth. But what a tooth! It measured six inches in length. Five minutes later I found my second tooth. Despite breathing nitrox, by then it was time to decompress. Pete and I ascended, and did half an hour of decompression.

The meteorologists fumbled the forecast. Fifteen-knot winds and moderating two-to-four foot seas grew worse instead of better. By half time (surface interval), the winds were up to twenty knots and the seas were four to five feet. We toughed it out.

Rob decided to look for a new location. He dived alone, pulled the hook, then dragged a buoy line around the bottom while scouting for another productive area. This time the depth was 110 feet. Again he returned with teeth. We live-boated instead of anchoring. Mike and Chris went down the buoy line, dragged it around with them, and brought back some more teeth.

Pete and I descended. The buoy weight had dragged across the bottom. We took the weight in hand and followed the drag mark until we found coral heads – a distance of several hundred feet. Pete spotted the first tooth exposed. So we hunkered down and commenced to dig in the locality. This time we did much better. I found nearly a dozen teeth ranging in size from three to four inches. Pete found a fossilized whale vertebra. Whale rib bones were scattered everywhere.

The water was warm (77° on the bottom, 83° on the

deco), calm, and ambient light visibility exceeded 25 feet. I was satisfied with the "take" from both dives. After another half hour of decompression, we surfaced into raging seas: honest six-footers that were steep and close together. Whitecaps were everywhere, making the sea look like surf, or perhaps a field of cotton that was waiting to be picked. It made for a tough ride home.

We stayed in our wetsuits. Rob and Pete took turns at the helm. At times the boat was airborne as it flew off a crest into a trough. Flying fish took wing at our approach. Dense spray struck me constantly in the face, and worked its way between my clenched lips. I found myself constantly spitting salt water from my mouth. We endured this torment for three solid hours. After twelve hours at sea in an open boat, I was totally exhausted.

But it was worth it!

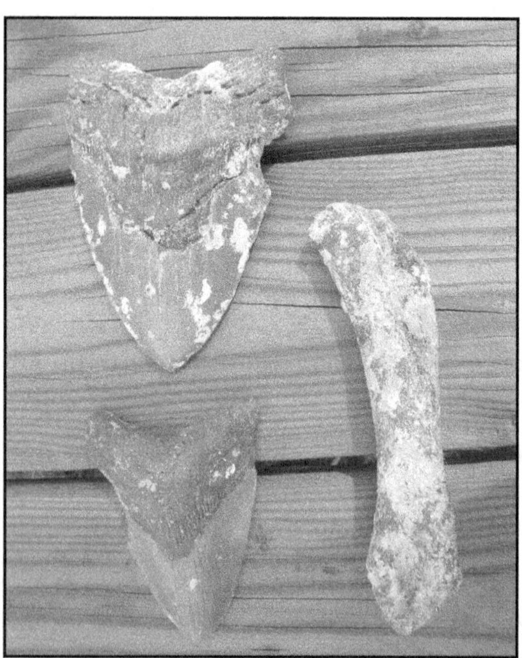

I saved the best for last. In the upper left is my six-inch meg tooth. The tooth in the lower left is in better condition, with more enamel and well-defined serrated edges. That's a bone on the right.

The Wreck of the Granny

One of my favorite poets is Robert W. Service. In addition to his serious work, he wrote such classics of comic poetry as "The Cremation of Sam McGee" and "The Shooting of Dan McGrew." I make no bones about emulating the style that he employed in these two masterpieces. The following poem is a homage that I composed for wreck-divers.

'Twas a dark and stormy night,
with the *Granny* traveling right
along the rollers of the deep blue sea;
With the crow's nest swinging way
above the salty spume and spray
like an eagle's aerie in a lofty tree.
The hatches were all battened,
and the passengers were flattened
In their bunks or praying down upon their knees,
For the forecast was portending
and the night was never-ending;
the barometer was dropping by degrees.
And the waves were cresting high
above the troughs, and bye and bye,
one did crash upon the deck abaft the peak.
Sending torrents of cold water
through the rivet holes and mortar.
Soon the decks and wooden hull began to leak.

The captain was awakened
from his berth when rudely shaken
by the mate who had the eight to midnight watch,
Who stood steadfast by the helmsman

as the spray had overwhelmed him,
and whose valor was impossible to match.
For he'd often stood in weather,
dressed from head to toe in leather,
braving elements and facing them alone;
Fearing not the peals of thunder
nor the lightning strikes asunder
nor the crashing seas that drenched him to the bone.
Now he faced the captain squarely
as he braced himself quite fairly
'tween the bulkhead and the cabin's swinging door.
And he uttered supplications
and he offered God oblations,
his hands folded and his knees upon the floor.

Then he told the captain clearly,
"Sir, I've done my best sincerely,
I have reefed the sails and tightened all the lines.
I have battened all the hatches
and I've double-checked the latches
and I've sealed the ports and lashed them down with twine.
I have put the men to pumping
all the holds, and they are dumping
excess baggage o'er the side to give us speed.
But the storm is so uncanny
that I fear the dear old *Granny*
cannot make the shore before the winds succeed.
For the masts are all a'swaying
and the livestock are a'braying,
and the passengers are saying we won't live.
Though the men are hard at caulking
and the bilge pumps are not balking,
still the hull is leaking like a blessed sieve."

So the captain stretched and yawned
and rubbed his eyes as if the dawn
had let the sunlight through the port while
starboard tacking,
As if the sea were calm and placid
and the air was not so acid
with the spark of ozone from the lightning
cracking,
As if the oakum were not leaking
and the timbers were not creaking
and the deck lights were not dimmed by frost
and foam,
As if the pitching and the rolling
and the bell that then was tolling
were the motions and the sounds of home sweet
home.
With one hand upon the scaling
bunk bed's twisted iron railing,
and the other combing whiskers from his lip,
The captain shook his snowy mane
and smoothed the beard on which he'd lain,
and listened to the creaks and groans within the
ship.

Now the captain was a man who'd
sailed the world and always viewed
the sea as good a home as sailors ever had,
Who'd learned his trade before the mast
and who'd been forced to grow up fast
as he had been at sea since he was but a lad;
Who'd spent his time the sails a'furling
when the waves were big and curling
while more timid boys lay down and hugged the
deck;
Who'd climbed the mizzen or the main
just so that he could feel the rain
beat out a tattoo on his head and on his neck;
Who'd cheer the tempest that was raging
in a voice that was engaging
and be heard above the mates who only cursed.

Who loved the ocean and its motion
and fell sway to no emotion
when the wind and waves combined to give their worst.

Now the captain was two-fisted,
and a brawler who desisted
never once from fights that often came his way.
He would rather kick and punch
than back down from a rowdy bunch
of seamen who let whiskey lead them all astray.
Who could win in any brawling,
who found storms at sea enthralling,
who embraced the waves as one might hug a lover.
Who'd sailed through typhoons full-sheeted,
who'd bucked snow and ice surfeited
with the power of his mastery all over.
So he stood upon his sea leg
and strapped on his hardwood peg leg,
and he pulled the mate erect by one slumped shoulder.
Then he dragged him from the cabin
while he commenced to shout and gab in
sailor's language that was spiced with words a'bolder.

"I have sailed before the mast
on ships that nearly breathed their last
in seven seas that stretched from Nice to Timbuktu;
Through nasty tropic hurricanes
and through the hard torrential rains
that burst the sails and snapped the masts and halyards, too.
Through winter snow and arctic ice
that scared the hands like they were mice,
through big typhoons that tore the rails and planks to kindling.
I defy the gods that beckon.

I won't be damned like Vanderdecken,
the Flying Dutchman who was only fair to
middling.
I will save the dear old *Granny*
though the weather be uncanny
and the Sirens sing entreaties from the islands.
For neither deity nor creature
is strong enough to make me beach her.
I will anchor in the shadow of the highlands."

Up on deck the wind was frightful,
and the captain had a sight full
through the telescoping spyglass held to
eyeball.
Land was peaking through the haze.
The rocks ahead were like a maze.
The captain sneered and sang a chantey
somewhat ribald.
He wrapped his fingers 'round a spoke,
and turned the helm that nearly broke
the rudder as it strained against the rudderpost.
And as the mate looked on aghast,
the captain peered around the mast
and shouted once again another vulgar boast,
Then swung his arm that had the hook,
around his head without a look,
and sank the point into the fife rail's forward
post.
One arm forward and one aft,
his body upright like a shaft,
he steered the *Granny* through the rocks and
toward the coast.

Wild surf then crashed across the peak.
The brine rolled down along the teak,
and sloshed around the legs of captain and his
mate.
The mate was washed across the deck
and caught a shroud around the neck,
but grabbed a marlinspike so didn't meet his fate.

The captain raised his wooden leg,
and stamped it down upon a peg
that held a deck plank to the timber underneath.
The treenail darted through the planking
with a squeal and with a clanking.
Now his leg was lodged in wood-to-wood relief.
He stood firm in this position
with his trussed up disposition
stretched from helm to post to deck: a three-point moor.
Then he turned the wheel of fate,
careened between the rocks of slate,
and cursed Poseidon with a rash stentorian roar.

The *Granny* bumped against a boulder,
but refused to wrack and molder,
then she shot ahead in wicked ricochet.
She rose up a crashing comber,
hit the trough like a dive-bomber,
and charged forward like the old mare tinted gray.
The captain cheered aloud forthrightly.
He ignored the waves that sprightly
smashed against the stem and washed away the hamper.
He gripped the helm with frigid fingers,
while torn chocks made perfect ringers
'round his peg leg that could not get any damper.
He steered a course past jutting headland,
saw a bay that rimmed the mainland,
then he spun the wheel aport and headed southward.
He passed a boulder that was pointed,
while the sea his head anointed.
He spit water, yelled he wasn't any coward.

The *Granny* struck a sandbar lightly,
shivered timbers that should rightly
have collapsed around his ears, but kept on standing.

Masts were shaken, shrouds were falling;
and the surf was most appalling,
yet he kept on course toward wharves where boats were landing.
The top yards snapped and broke asunder,
and it was quite a little wonder
that the *Granny* didn't founder in the bay.
The halyards fell across the skylight,
blocks and tackle no more upright,
and one hawser snapped, its anchor not aweigh.
The reefed sails then commenced to flapping,
and the deadeyes started rapping
on the hull where all the chainplates were now straining.
Some planks were sprung, the hull was leaking,
and the holds were rank and reeking,
and the water in the bilge was slowly gaining.

Then came the final fearful moment,
when the breakers dared to foment
trouble that an average skipper would abhor.
The captain mocked the gods and laughed,
ignored the swaying booms and gaff,
and toward an empty wharf the wrecked windjammer bore.
The jibboom drove across the landing
with loose canvas still expanding
from the gale that struck the *Granny* from astern.
The bowsprit chains lassoed a bollard,
so the forward end was collared;
now the broadside struck the piles from stem to stern.
The mainmast gave a final shudder,
and the shock unshipped the rudder,
while the crow's nest took a nosedive to the dock.
The shrouds then tangled 'round a cleat,
the bights belayed so nice and neat
that the longshoremen just backed away in shock.

The captain let go of the spoke,
reached in his pocket for a smoke,
and pulled his peg leg like a dowel from its hole.
He freed his hook from fife rail post,
surveyed the wreckage and almost
guffawed again at gods that dared defy his role.
The mate regained his unshod feet,
the crew commenced to dance and bleat,
While the passengers crept up from decks below.
The captain lighted his clay pipe,
puffed smoke until the air was ripe,
and displayed calm, as if he fared a minor blow.
He merely stood in self-reliance,
didn't shout his loud defiance,
for once the *Granny* was in harbor, he was bored.
He had one thought upon his mind:
to go to sea, to brawl, unwind,
and to embrace the call that only *he* adored.

Blurbs and Forewords

During my auctorial career I have written or dictated all kinds of oddments, from newspaper and magazine fillers to book blurbs and forewords, plus legal briefs and court reports.

My praise for the works of other authors is sincere. I have a strict policy in this regard: if I didn't like the manuscript in question, I would return payment rather than write something that was either negative or dishonest.

A negative blurb or foreword would never be used by the author or publisher. A dishonest blurb or foreword would not only go against my grain, but would abuse my reputation to lend credibility that was undeserved.

Here is a sampling of these recent shorter pieces.

Scuba Diving the Wrecks and Shores of Long Island, NY

by David Rosenthal

(foreword)

The spirit of adventure is alive and well.

This fact may not be apparent to people whose only view of events emanates from newspapers or television: media that thrive on murder and mayhem. As David Rosenthal's book clearly demonstrates, the instinctive drive that led mankind to leave his cave to search far and wide, to sail tempestuous seas, to cross vast forests and plains, to climb tall mountains, and to venture into the ocean's depths, is still a motivating force in certain individuals.

Whereas some people are merely passing through

life, David and others like him are embracing the unknown experiences that make life exciting. His adventures in deep waters, and in long-distance penetrations into the cavernous hull of the *San Diego*, are only the obvious parts of the story that his book relates: the sweet icing on a rich cake that is multi-layered and made from many esoteric ingredients.

Certainly this book is about exploration. But it is about more than the investigation of sunken and collapsing shipwrecks: it is about the examination of the inner self. On the surface, the narrative hook appears to be about problems that are encountered, confronted, and overcome in a hostile environment in which death is literally only a breath away. In a broader sense, the book probes the subtle determination of people who seek somewhat risky activities not because they enjoy the feeling of fear and the rush of adrenaline, but because they possess an unquenchable desire to learn about their reactions to situations of stress. They can then be better prepared to anticipate and modify those reactions when similar circumstances recur during future emergencies.

If this analogy sounds tautological – like pursuing danger for the sake of pursuing more danger – then you are misreading my intent. An encounter with the unknown will strengthen the soul when the person takes the trouble to analyze the encounter. Honest analysis makes a person stronger than he was before the encounter. Additional encounters enable a person to flex and exercise his intellectual might – in short, to grow emotionally. Facing perils and overcoming them is a way to build character and self-confidence.

Because bottom time is limited by air supply, a diver needs to heighten his powers of observation and perception. Learning to think quickly and to retain fleeting images are essential. The deeper one descends into the dark abyss, the quicker one must be able to react "under pressure."

People dive – and dive deep – for different reasons. For me the reasons are the challenges that are presented and the adventures that ensue. After reading David's book, I suspect that he and I have similar philosophies. The following book is about people who dare to do what others only dream about.

Victoria's Ships' Graveyard

by Mark Ryan et al

(foreword)

If you are wondering why an American wreck-diver is furnishing a foreword for a book on Australian shipwrecks, the explanation is quite simple. Mark Ryan, one of the authors, acted as my tour guide during one of my sojourns to the land down under.

Mark did not know me when I visited Melbourne, yet he graciously volunteered to escort me through the J-class submarines. Those were experiences that I will treasure forever. He also took me on a drift dive through the harbor entrance.

My short stay convinced me that I had touched only the tip of the local wreck-diving iceberg. Had I spent weeks or months in town, I doubt that I could have dived on all the wrecks that litter the seabed within easy reach of Melbourne. There were so many more wrecks to see, and so little time . . .

Mark's familiarity with the submarines made our penetrations seem easy – deceptively easy. And therein lies the rub.

The key phrase in wreck-diving – and particularly in deep wreck-diving – is "risk management." Even shallow wrecks can be dangerous, especially during penetration into dark interior spaces. One can get lost or entangled, or suffer a variety of equipment malfunctions. The deeper the wreck, the more hazardous it becomes: bottom time is short, and nitrogen narcosis lingers on the fringe of perceptibility. Effective decompression is always problematical.

The true wreck-diver will not be deterred by the perils that are inherent in the activity. Instead, he will learn to handle stress and deal with uncommon situations. Then he will proceed with caution.

By its very nature, exploration entails confrontation with the unknown. To me, it is this unknown quantity that is the seductive attraction of wreck-diving. After a lifetime spent in the pursuit of shipwrecks, I still feel the thrill of excitement as I descend the anchor line to a wreck that I haven't dived before.

I would write more, but it is time to go diving . . .

Islands in the Sand

by Charlie Hudson

(cover blurb)

Charlie Hudson has written a book that is long overdue. *Islands in the Sand* is a lucid account of the history and the importance of artificial reefs. She has done her homework. Fascinating facts and background detail are spiced with informative interviews with people who have conceptualized, designed, manufactured, or deployed various forms of manmade marine habitats. Her compelling treatment examines these burgeoning oases from a variety of angles, giving readers the multifaceted viewpoints of the main beneficiaries: anglers, divers, scientists, anyone who cares about the environment, and the creatures that take residence in their newfound abode. She clearly demonstrates why artificial reefs are for the betterment of all. Her lyric prose is a testament to modern educational theory, proving elegantly that one can both instruct and entertain at the same time.

Lost Chapters from Shipwrecks of New York

When I pasted up the manuscript for Shipwrecks of New York, *I discovered that the book exceeded its anticipated length. I had covered too many shipwrecks. Because of printing costs, the way to maintain the uniform cover price of $20 for each volume of the Popular Dive Guide Series was to keep the page allowance at 240 pages.*

Out of economic necessity, I was forced to delete eight chapters. I chose to delete those wrecks that were of lesser interest to wreck-divers (my primary targeted audience). I hated to do this because these wrecks were of historic importance to armchair explorers and local interest readers. These stories are tragic and full of pathos.

This book gives me the opportunity to resurrect the lost chapters.

Ajace

Built: 1872 Sunk: March 4, 1881
Previous names: None Depth: 25 feet
Gross tonnage: 566 Dimensions: 144' x 32' x 19'
Type of vessel: Wooden-hulled bark Power: Sail
Builder: Bruzzone, in Voltri, Italy
Owner: E.E. Zino
Port of registry: Genoa, Italy
Cause of sinking: Ran Aground
Location: 26956.6 43754.1

At least one American reporter did not think much of the seaworthiness of the bark *Ajace*. He wrote in the *New York Times*, "Like most of the Italian vessels, she was a clumsy-looking vessel and a very slow sailor. She left Antwerp, in ballast, on the 17th of December, bound for this port. Sixty days is an average passage, and the *Ajace* had been out nearly 80. It is recorded that one of these Italian tubs has occupied 180 days in the passage across the Atlantic."

Although I have been unable to locate a photograph or illustration of the *Ajace*, the above reportage can be discounted in at least one detail: the bark was not in ballast, although her cargo was very light. Elsewhere it was written, "The *Ajace* was consigned to Seager Brothers, shipping merchants, of No. 63 Beaver-street. By them she was loaded with 36,428 bushels of grain, and was sent to Antwerp, sailing from this port on the 31st of August. She was on her way back to receive another cargo of grain when she was wrecked. She had on board 2,040 empty petroleum barrels, valued at about $3,000, which were owned by Gustave Heye, of No. 138 Pearl-street, and a small quantity of railroad iron, worth about $2,000. The *Ajace* was valued at about $15,000."

The winter weather in Europe may have been mild when the *Ajace* left Belgium in late December, but by the time of her arrival off the American coast, Long Island was shuddering under the vehement forces of nature. A March gale was pounding coastal communities with unrelenting fury. According to the Life-Saving Service report, "By midnight the storm had fairly set in. By 2 o'clock there was a roaring gale, the sea had grown terrific and, through an atmosphere of dense fog, the rain fell in torrents. At half-past 7 o'clock on the morning of the 4th, the gale had reached its height, and, in the judgment of the most experienced surfmen, was blowing at the rate of fifty miles an hour. It was not until near 11 o'clock that the fog lifted and the storm broke. In the meantime, the damage had been immense all along the coast. Many vessels that had sought a harbor in Raritan Bay were washed into the meadows, swamped or sunk, and at various points along shore wrecks were frequent. At Long Branch the ravage was considerable. In many places the bluff was cut away by the breakers. About a thousand feet of bulkhead were washed out, and a section of the outer end of the iron pier, about ten feet wide and twenty feet long, with an iron girder weighing twenty-five hundred pounds, was wrenched off, and despite its ponderous bulk carried up on to the beach. At Coney Island, there was savage havoc. For several years the tide had not been so high, and the furious water tore away the Plymouth Rock pier, broke down and demolished one side of the Hussey Hotel, swept off most of the Tilyon bathing-houses, left the Marine Railway station not much better than a ruin, damaged the entire railroad track, and wrought mischief to the extent of many thousands of dollars.

"At about 9 o'clock on the morning of the 4th, although the gale was still violent, the rain falling hard and thick, and the surf and sea tremendous, the storm had passed its height and was beginning to break, a fact evidenced by the shifting of the heavy fog, which at moments fell away, sometimes half a mile, sometimes even two miles, allowing a view of the ocean to those distances. In one of the farthest of these recessions of vapor, at the hour above named, the crew of Life-Saving Station No. 36, (Third District,) who were out on the beach at Rockaway, saw a bark standing directly toward the station, under close-reefed topsails, about two miles away. Her navigators appeared to suddenly discover her proximity to the shore, for she was abruptly hauled around to the southward and westward, and went pitching and tossing along the outer edge of Rockaway Shoals, which were on her lee. The flood-tide was then setting in to New York Bay, and the heave of the sea seemed to make the bark sag rapidly to leeward. Presently she reached the point of the shoals, and they suddenly saw her topmasts fall alongside, which showed that she had struck bottom. The life-saving crew instantly sprang for the surf-boat, and, as the raging breakers made a launch in front of the station impossible, they hauled the boat over to the bay in the rear of the beach, somewhat over half a mile distant, where the water was still, launched and rowed down through the inlet, hoping that there might be an opening out over the bar; but the sea was a stupendous mass of foam as far as the eye could reach, and the breakers spread across the bar in an incessant tumbling wall. As the ebbing of the tide, by abating the surf, might give them the opportunity they sought, the men remained on their oars at the mouth of the inlet until 2 o'clock in the afternoon watching the foggy offing. No effort, however, appeared to be demanded of them, for nothing could now be seen of the bark, and finally the men naturally supposed that, after striking, she had worked off the shoals and proceeded on her way.

"They were mistaken, and a terrible catastrophe had happened. The bark they had seen was the *Ajace*, of Genoa, Italy, 566 tons register, Federico Morice, master, bound from Antwerp, Belgium, for New York, laden with old iron and empty kerosene barrels. She had fourteen men on board, including the captain, of whom only one was destined to survive her destruction. It appears from the story of this man, Pietro Sala, an Austrian, that at the time the bark was seen by the crew of No. 36, she was driving in the northeast gale, all sign of land being hidden by the fog. Without any premonition, she suddenly struck the shoal on her starboard side with a shock so dreadful as to demolish her steering gear. The waves at once burst over her and began to rend her to pieces. For about three-quarters of an hour she resisted the process of demolition. Her crew meanwhile gathered at the stern, around the deck-cabin. They had fallen almost immediately into utter despair. The survivor, who seemed to have preserved his coolness better than the others, states that they stood loudly praying to the Madonna, a picture of whom one of them, the steward, held in his hands. In the midst of the tumult of supplications, Sala saw the carpenter cutting his throat with a knife, and immediately after the steward and two others also drew their knives and slashed their necks savagely. The four men did not die or fall from their wounds, but stood on the convulsed deck loudly raving out their prayers, with the blood spouting from the gashes. A few minutes later Sala had gone into the cabin, when the hull lifted and fell with a tremendous shock, and the ship tumbled to pieces. He found himself among fragments of planking and timber, and sprang to the air-hole of the cabin to climb out upon the roof; an effort in which he succeeded. The cabin had been torn from the hull with the after part of the spar-deck, to which it had been attached, and was floating, with a few feet of the mizzen-mast and top mast sticking up through the wreck, the lower part of the mast having slipped down through. The ship had entirely disappeared. In the dense enclosure of fog, through which streamed a mighty wind, nothing could be seen from the almost submerged raft on which the sailor lay clinging, but some ten feet equidistance of foaming green swells, strewn all over with a pell-mell of tumbling barrels and shattered planks and beams. Presently, amidst this confusion, Sala saw the third officer and two men with bloody throats rise from the water alongside his square of wreck, clutching it in a frantic effort to gain its summit. The third officer, a young Italian, and one of the men fell backward in a few minutes, unable to maintain their hold, and were engulfed. The other, who was the carpenter, a robust young man, struggled longer, and even got within reach of Sala, who seized him and tried to haul him up, but the strength of the bleeding wretch seemed to suddenly give way, and he hung inertly on the edge of the roof until his weight dragged him from the hands that held him, and he fell away and went down. Sala remained alone upon the cabin top, drifting he knew not whither.

"In the meantime the hurricane was raging in its dying fury along the shore of Coney Island, and all the beach resounded with the crash and shock of ponderous breakers, flung down incessantly with a noise like that of great cliffs falling. The frail bridge which connected the Nereid boat-house itself, standing on a pile foundation, was in such danger, under the buffeting wind and flooding sea, that Keeper Charles Bebensee, of Life-Saving Station No. 37, (Coney Island), went out with his crew in the surf-boat, and brought ashore from the building a man and a woman, who were there in great peril. Between 10 and 11 o'clock in the forenoon the fog began to roll back over the waste of wild and crested water, and Keeper Bebensee, who was on the beach, saw a dark mass, which he at first took for a portion of an old dock or wharf, rising and falling aslant upon the foaming swells, every other moment dropping from sight into the trough of the seas. He brought his marine-glass to bear upon it, and made out the after house or cabin of a vessel, and a stump of a mast and top-mast sticking up through it, together with a man clinging to the top of the house, feebly waving his cap. It was the survivor of the *Ajace*. The surf-boat was at once launched by Keeper Bebensee and his crew, and amidst roaring cheers from the assemblage on the beach, several hundred persons, mostly workmen on the neighboring hotels, having gathered, a splendid struggle with the sea was entered upon. It seemed impossible that any boat could live, still less make headway, against the enormous bursts of surf that barred the way, and it was literally inch by inch that the passage through the breakers was effected. All the powers of the agile surf-boat had to be brought into their wariest exercise by the life-saving crew to prevent an overturn, while it was only by the sternest toil of the oarsmen that any advance could be made against the heavy inshore rush of the combers. Each moment of the contest was big with peril, and when the breakers were at length passed, and the boat was rising and falling like a chip on the vast toppling swells of the outer sea, this peril seemed so much increased that the crowd on shore, who had long maintained their cheers of enthusiasm and crew of encouragement, gradually grew still and watched mutely, with pale faces, the gallant crew, as they strained their oars with desperate courage against the surge, steadily aiming for the fragment of the wreck on which lay the half inanimate seaman. Although this waif was only about a mile and a half from land when first discerned, the perils and difficulties of the passage were so great that it took a full hour for the boat to come within hailing distance. It was seen upon approach that the cabin, upon which the sailor lay, was attached to the deck and deck-beams, and it required skilful manoeuvering to keep the surf-boat from being struck by these projections as they rose from their submersion on the swells. By combined management and daring, the keeper and his men shot up alongside, and, as it were, snatched off the benumbed and exhausted seaman, whose joy at his deliverance was almost delirious. The boat was then headed around for her perilous voyage back to the beach, where, after an hour's struggle, it arrived in safety, amidst the wildest cheering from the people who had witnessed this laborious and gallant rescue. With the assistance of the eager crowd, the life-saving crew lifted and carried to the station the now almost insensible body of the only man saved from the demolished vessel. Restoratives being administered, and every necessary attention being given, he soon recovered from his terrible experience, and took dinner with the men; after which, as well as his broken English would allow, he told his story, which was subsequently obtained in a clearer form in a deposition taken before the Italian consul. The material facts have been recited here.

"It is manifest that this was a case of shipwreck occurring almost beyond the province of the Life-Saving Service, and that no human aid could, under the circumstances, have reached any of the unfortunate crew, except the single man providentially drifted near enough to the beach to become the subject of a daring and dangerous effort to save him – an effort which happily succeeded."

One body, unidentified, washed onto the beach later in the day, as did the section of the poop deck on which Sala had ridden through the waves, the latter coming to rest "less than a hundred yards from the east end of the Brighton Bathing Pavilion, the starboard side of the cabin forming an acute angle with the line of the Marine Railway. Another fragment, a part of the deck over the forecastle, with the capstan attached, drifted ashore about 200 yards west of Manhattan Beach Hotel. Halfway between these pieces of the wreck is the principal part of the mainmast – about 40 feet of the lower part – lying high and dry at the base of the Marine Railway road-bed. The bulk of the wreck, half buried in the sand upon the extreme point of Rockaway Reef, could be distinctly seen with the naked eye at low tide yesterday from the door of the Life-saving Station. Several sloops were anchored nearby and by the aid of a glass swarms of wreckers could be distinctly seen stripping it of everything of value. A large number of wreckers – members of the independent brigade – were also busy all day stripping the fragments of the wreck upon the Coney Island beach of every piece of metal exposed to view. Half a dozen of them pried the capstan from its fastenings and carried it away. Nothing else of value except the capstan is yet known to have drifted ashore. True, a rumor was afloat that several hundred dollars in bills had been found on the beach, but this could not be traced to any authentic source. Some fragments of sails and rigging were also picked up and carried off by land pirates."

The above description gives the reader an idea of how much – or how little – of the *Ajace* might possibly remain, especially after so many years of storms and strong currents. Little more than the keel and the bottom of the hull are likely to mark the site of so dreadful a catastrophe.

Despite the gruesome horror of death and suffering, the wreck of the *Ajace* immediately became a busy tourist attraction. "Hundreds of people went down to the beach during the day, many of them from this City and Brooklyn. The number of ladies and children was remarkable. Many of the ladies were in seal-skin sacques. 'We have had a good deal of travel to-day,' said Conductor Hemstead, of the Prospect Park and Coney Island Railroad, to a reporter of The Times, 'and tomorrow we expect to have a good deal more, and will run special trains.' "

The next day people thronged to the site of the disaster, some in "public hacks" and others in "private equipages." Reported the *New York Times*, "Early in the afternoon there must have been several thousand people on the island. The 2:30 o'clock train on the Prospect Park and Coney Island Railroad carried 465 persons, and the 4 o'clock train 285 more. Of course, a good many Brooklynites drove down to the island by the Boulevard in their own conveyances.

"The centre of attraction for everybody was, as may be imagined, the fragments of the wrecked *Ajace* which have drifted ashore. The poop deck, which, with the cabin house and a part of the mizzenmast standing, lies high and dry upon the beach, within a stone's throw of the east end of the Brighton Beach Bathing Pavilion, was surrounded – in fact, covered – all day long by a relic-seeking crowd. Men, women, and children crowded, elbowed, and actually squeezed each other in the open parallelogram which had formerly been inclosed by the cabin walls. Men and boys climbed in scores upon the cabin roof; amateur sailors clambered up the splintered mizzenmast, and everybody, without regard to age, sex, or condition of physical strength, was tugging with might and main to break off a fragment of the wreck. From a distance the wreck had the appearance of an ant-hill with great black ants swarming over it. The veneering of white pine with which what remained of the sides of the cabin was lined, was stripped off, broken into fragments, and distributed among the friends of the fortunate possessors. The men who climbed the mizzenmast broke off the splinters at the top and threw them down. Others stood upon the cabin-roof and carefully subdivided and passed the fragments around. Some men had blacksmith's hammers with which they knocked off bolts and eyes and rings and then started for home rejoicing. It was asserted, on the basis of a careful estimate made by an experienced railroad man, that the Prospect Park and Coney Island Railroad Company transported about three tons of free freight to the City yesterday in the way of relics."

Most of the empty barrels rolled around in the surf until they were rescued and carted off by souvenir hunters. Five more bodies came ashore in the ensuing days, including that of Captain Federico Morice, master of the *Ajace*.

Prior to the inquest, allegations were made that the captain and crew were drunk prior to the stranding, that Sala was guilty of murder and not some crew members of suicide, and that $2,500 in specie was locked up in the captain's cabin, but nothing could be substantiated since every fact concerning the wreck must necessarily have come from the sole survivor, Pietro Sala. Suspicions grew when Sala could not be found at the sailor's boarding house on Water Street, where he had been put up, when he was called to testify at the inquest. However, his absence was only temporary, and he had not left the country aboard a foreign vessel, as some accused him of doing in order to escape punishment for imaginary wrongdoings. He later testified in broken English (Sala was Austrian) to the satisfaction of Justice John McMahon and the jury, which returned a verdict of accidental drowning. "A slight wound was found in the throat of one of the men, but as it was not sufficient to cause death the general verdict met the case, so that the theory of suicide was not maintained. The bodies were buried at the expense of the Italian government."

Today the wreck is also buried, although at nature's expense. Very little can be seen protruding from the sand except a few worm-eaten timbers and part of the cargo of railroad iron. For the patient diver who spends the time to fan off the upper grains, there may be more to be found.

The *Ajace* is known locally as the Italian.

Arlington

Built: 1883 Sunk: August 17, 1909
Previous names: None Depth: Unknown
Gross tonnage: 592 Dimensions: 144' x 34' x 17'
Type of vessel: Wooden hulled, 3-masted schooner
Builder: William H. Genn & Company, Bucksport, Maine
Owner: John S. Emery & Company, Boston, Massachusetts Power: Sail
Port of registry: Boston, Massachusetts
Cause of sinking: Ran aground
Location: 3/4 miles east of Long Beach Life-Saving Station

The *Arlington* began her career rigged as a barkentine. She was the last vessel built in the private shipyard of William H. Genn, which he had established in 1874, at a time when the construction of sailing ships was a major industry in Maine. For more than a quarter of a century the *Arlington* served admirably in American coastal waters; her flapping canvas was a common sight along the continent's eastern shore. Like the majority of the sailing freighters of the sea, she made little or no media impact until she met her untimely demise on the south shore of Long Island. By that time her yards had been removed and her rig had been converted to that of a schooner, probably because schooners did not require as large a crew to spread their sails as did barkentines. Even in the days of low wages, a man-hour saved was a man-hour additional profit for the owners.

On her final voyage she was bound from Boston to Mayville, Florida, with a cargo of coal worth $2,050. The value of the *Arlington* was given as $10,000. For three days she sailed uneventfully, under the command of Captain Ira Small and with a stalwart crew of eight. Instead of a dull passage which was the norm for a coastal coaling schooner, the sailors on board had the experience of a lifetime and a close call with death.

Although the photograph of the *Arlington* stranded beyond the breakers, with the crew coming ashore in a surfboat, evokes dramatic imagery of what heroic efforts must have been expended by the members of the life-saving service, the official report of the stranding and rescue is tantalizingly laconic and understated.

"Surfman on watch discovered her, and the life-saving crew made several unsuccessful attempts to land her crew with the beach apparatus. Assisted by the Point Lookout crew they then manned the surfboat and succeeded in getting out to her through the high surf. The 8 men on board were brought ashore in safety. One other man, who had drifted to sea on some wreckage early in the morning, was picked up off Seabright, N.J., the following day by a fishing schooner; 2 of the men rescued were helpless from exposure, but were revived by the use of stimulants, hot-water bags, etc. The men were all furnished dry clothing. The vessel became a total loss."

Fortunately, newspaper accounts of the incident

The rescue of the men from the *Arlington*. (From Harper's Weekly.)

were more detailed. In mid-August 1909, a fierce storm swept the coast with winds in excess of fifty miles per hour. Into this tempest Captain Small had the temerity to sail. But instead of heading south on her intended course, tacking against the wind, the *Arlington* was blown uncontrollably northward, forcing the captain to swing her around and run close-hauled with shortened sails until she found herself on the breakers in front of the Nassau Hotel at Long Beach.

Enjoying the storm in an early version of a "hurricane party" were four hundred guests who, instead of lazing about the beach collecting a tan as they would like to have been doing, were confined to the premises in utter boredom – until the morning of the seventeenth, when the *Arlington* came ashore practically under their windows.

In the first wee hours of darkness, none on shore knew of the *Arlington's* precarious situation. Captain Small "felt his vessel strike three times. Then the rudder was carried away. The big inrolling seas continued to bump the *Arlington* along up the shelving ocean floor for about three times her length. Then she stuck fast, and they continued to break over her, many reaching as high as the beam of the mizzen mast."

With the bow pointing toward shore and the stern taking the brunt of the sea, she soon swung partly about. The nine men on deck raced forward, away from the crashing waves. They clambered out onto the bowsprit, which angled upward and away from the spuming cauldron below, and clung to the stays to await their fate. No sooner had they arrived than "the whole after deck 'blew out.' Either the air between the cargo and the deck became overcompressed by the entrance of water through a leak or some of the gases from her cargo of coal siftings were released. At any rate, with the blowing open of the deck a great hole was quickly beaten in the *Arlington's* ocean-ward side."

It was at this point that the *Arlington* was sighted by Charles Helmcke, a member of the Long Beach Life-Saving Station whose job was to patrol the beach that night in the fierce storm. "Through the driving mist he caught a glimpse of the small light at the vessel's tossing peak. Looking closer he made out the nine figures clinging to the bowsprit. He shot off the two red coston lights which he carried, to show the sailors he had seen them. Then he ran back to the station and roused Capt. Langdon and his dozen men.

"Trundling their Lyle brass swivel gun and carrying under their arms the long cartridges, containing the three-quarter inch wire lines, the life savers ran down the beach to a point opposite the wreck, immediately underneath the windows of the big Summer hotel. Their first and second shots fell short. Then there was a long wait while the ill-aimed lines were recoiled. A third shot was finally fired, and the line fell across the schooner's head stays. Capt. Small seized it, and, with the united strength of all his men, tried to drag it in.

"But the undertow was too strong, and even the efforts of the eight sailors could not pull after it the bigger rope which was attached to it. Their efforts were not very enthusiastic anyhow, Capt. Small pointing out later that neither he nor his men would have dared sit in a breeches buoy, the cable for which was attached so low. The only place they could have tied the cable to would have been the bowsprit, and the buoy and the man in it would have had to travel practically the whole 300 yards to shore under water."

One sailor, Mans Pierson, decided to take his fate into his own hands. "Seeing a nine-foot section of the smashed decking float beneath him, with an inarticulate shout to his comrades he dropped fifteen feet into the ocean and gripped the planks. He was seen to climb partially up on the decking. Then he disappeared in the mist."

It was the gunshots which aroused the late sleepers at the Nassau Hotel, now bathed by the rays of the sun as the early morning mist burned away. The sight that greeted them moved them to pity, and many complained that the life-savers were not doing enough to effect the rescue of the beleaguered sailors clinging desperately to the bowsprit.

But the life-savers knew their job and went about it professionally. They returned to the station and "half dragged, half floated the big lifeboat down the beach. Amid cheers from the hotel guests the life savers ran their boat out into the ocean at about 8:30 o'clock, over four hours after the first sighting of the wreck. The tide was at its lowest, and in the mountainous seas the whaleboat at first seemed merely to be bobbing up and down. But finally, when the lifeboat had come as close as it dared beneath the waving bowsprit, the hotel folk on the boardwalk saw Capt. Small tie the 'whip' of the wire buoy line around the small body of the negro cabin boy. The boy was passed back into the whaleboat's stern, and the wire was untied and dragged back. The Captain tied it around the small, crouching form of the humpbacked Mexican cook. Then, after a pause, he did something which made the business men on the boardwalk raise an expostulating shout and their wives to cry out in terror.

"He was seen to strike the humpback repeatedly, and, finally, with a great effort, wrench him from the bowsprit and hurl him into the ocean. He was hauled safely aboard the whaleboat, however, and it turned out later that he had become partially paralyzed by exposure and could not release his stiffened hands from the rigging he clutched. He lay unconscious all day in the life-saving station, but revived at night. So risky was the proximity of the waving bowsprit that it took a full hour before the eight men could be lowered from it and passed over the life savers' shoulders into the whaleboat."

Hotel personnel took up a collection among the guests and raised $550 for the sailors who had lost everything in the wreck. The fourteen-year-old cabin boy was feted by the women who "took turns taking him to the shops in the hotel's arcade and buying him sweetmeats." It developed that at the tender age of twelve he had stowed away on the *Arlington*, was discovered, and, Captain Small feeling sorry for him and taking a liking to him, made him his cabin boy.

But the *Arlington's* story did not end that day, for there was still the strange odyssey of Mans Pierson, who was last seen drifting away from the wreck on a section of planking. Despite what his companions believed, he had not jumped from the bowsprit into the sea, but fell. "I remember coming up and looking toward the wreck, and then the wreckage came by me and I grabbed it and climbed up on it. I found the rope attached to it, and I picked up a long piece of planking that drifted down upon me. While I was making myself fast the board drifted away from the schooner. I never had any hope of making shore, but I believed that I would be able to bring up somewhere near Sandy Hook. It was the finding of that rope that saved my life, for I would never have been able to keep on the wreckage had I not been lashed to it.

"All that day I drifted - where I did not know – paddling ever in the direction where I thought the Jersey coast lay. A steamer bound in passed me. I shouted and waved my shirt. It got so cold that I had to put the shirt on again. Later in the day another vessel passed and again I signaled with my shirt. 'I won't give up,' I kept repeating, and though I saw other vessels I kept on repeating 'I won't give up.' Then I signaled them and kept on paddling. I never gave in, but I tell you I was pretty near it when, as darkness came, I heard in the distance the rattle of an anchor chain. I had an idea then where I was, for I knew that it must be some craft coming to anchor for the night. Near Sandy Hook. This I was sure of when a large steamship passed so far off that I could only get a glimmer of her lights, and she, too, came to anchor. Then came the flash of a light, and I renewed my paddling. I got to within 500 yards of the Highland Light when the tide caught me, and I was carried off my course, drifting southward and off shore. How I wanted a drink during the night."

Pierson spotted sixteen vessels in all, and all to no avail. Finally, after twenty-seven hours adrift, came his salvation. "Pierson's real rescuer was Sport, the spaniel mascot of the *Irene May.* For an hour before the wrecked sailor was sighted Sport had been running from one side of the craft to the other, sniffing to seaward and barking. This caused the skipper to keep a sharp lookout and presently he sighted Pierson two miles away. Capt. Ericsson at first thought he was a buoy adrift." The fishing schooner was on route from the fishing grounds off the coast of Maryland to New York harbor. "Once on board he drank four cups of coffee, ate a good meal and then borrowed a pipe and tobacco from one of the crew. But for sore feet he was none the worse for his long trip adrift."

Thus after great duress and dire exposure, all of the *Arlington's* crew were safe. Today, only a few scattered ribs in the sand remain to mark the annals of another day in the life of the valiant men of the Life-Saving Service, and the fortuitous survival of the ship's entire crew.

Bessie A. White

Built: 1919 Sunk: February 6, 1922
Previous names: None Depth: Unknown
Gross tonnage: 694 Dimensions: 182' x 37' x 12'
Type of vessel: Wooden-hulled, 4-masted schooner
Power: Sail with auxiliary gasoline engine
Builder: C.T. White & Son, Ltd., Alma, New Brunswick
Owner: C.T. White & Son, Ltd., Alma, New Brunswick
Port of registry: Parrsborough, Nova Scotia.
Cause of sinking: Ran aground
Location: Outer bar, one mile west of Smith's Point

One of the disadvantages that sailing ships have with respect to powered vessels is restricted maneuverability, especially when entering a crowded port against adverse winds and tides. For that reason, after the heyday of the windjammers yielded to the more reliable and economical steamships and their descendants, motor vessels, schooners were often equipped with auxiliary engines, not only to assist in docking and in moving away from wharves, but to add some speed during times of light wind. Thus the *Bessie A. White* was fitted with a gasoline engine and her wooden hull was pierced by a propeller shaft. The 6-cylinder engine was built by Wolverine Company of Boston, Massachusetts; it developed a meager fifty-seven horsepower.

In 1915, the United States Life-Saving Service was merged with the United States Revenue Cutter Service, and became known by the name which is today famous throughout the world: the United States Coast Guard. The old life-saving stations became Coast Guard stations. So on February 6, 1922, it was coastguardsmen who rendered aid when the *Bessie A. White* came to grief, in an incident whose retelling is all too brief.

"A lifeboat, in which Captain L.T. Merrian and three members of the crew were coming ashore, capsized, and James Rynburgh, a seaman, was almost drowned.

The schooner was bound for her home port, having left Newport News last Friday loaded with 1,500 tons of coal. At 4:30 the bow of the schooner stuck fast in a sand bar, almost opposite Bellport, and within 300 feet of the Smith's Point Coast Guard Station. The crew, three officers and six seamen, remained aboard for three hours, while the water deepened in the hold, and then set out in two lifeboats for the shore. The first boat, containing five men, reached land safely, but the second capsized in two feet of water 100 feet from shore. James Rynburgh, seaman, a Norwegian, was caught under the boat and was unconscious before the other three men were able to right it. Later he was revived and hurried to the Long Island College Hospital. Seven feet of water has now seeped into the hold of thc schooner, and it is thought that if a storm arises she may break in two."

If the bleached timbers of the *Bessie A. White* still reside on the bottom off Smith's Point, they must be either buried or heavily encrusted.

Bessie A. White. (From the author's collection.)

Charles E. Dunlap

Built: 1904 Sunk: July 22, 1919
Previous names: *Myrtle Tunnel, Forest City*
Gross tonnage: 1,294 Dimensions: 219' x 41' x 19'
Type of vessel: 5-masted schooner Power: Sail
Builder: Warren Sawyer, Millbridge, Maine
Owner: The Paulsen Company Depth: Unknown
Port of registry: San Juan, Puerto Rico
Cause of sinking: Ran aground
Location: Far Rockaway

The *Charles E. Dunlap* was built at a time when the sailing fleet was on the wane. At that time she was known as the *Myrtle Tunnel*, and sported only four masts. Her original home port was Savannah, Georgia. In 1907 her name was changed to *Forest City*. Then, in 1916, she was severely damaged by fire in Puerto Rico. When she was rebuilt in San Juan another mast was added to help increase her speed and, hopefully, her

Charles E. Dunlap as the *Myrtle Tunnel*. (From the author's collection.)

Courtesy of the Suffolk County Historical Society.

competitive edge. At least she avoided the ignominy of being dismasted and converted to a schooner barge, which happened to so many of her contemporaries. The *Forest City* was reborn from the fire as the *Charles E. Dunlap.*

The circumstances of her stranding were minor and non-dramatic and, fortunately, without any loss of life. Captain Richard Cropsie, master of the *Charles E. Dunlap*, "mistook the Rockaways for Coney island. He thought he was running in deep water between Coney Island and Sandy Hook."

Wrote the *New York Times*, "The heavy seas beating constantly upon her sides have opened large seams in the hull. It now appears that it will be impossible to pull her off the bar without the water pouring through the openings and sinking her. Lighters are standing by, and the cargo, machinery, sails, and everything of value that can be removed are being taken off the schooner. Only the hull of the vessel will be lost." In this case, machinery does not refer to propelling machinery, but rather to auxiliary machinery such as that needed to operate capstans and winches.

A wreck that might possibly be the *Charles E. Dunlap* has been reported in 25 feet of water at loran coordinates 26929.8 and 43755.2. It is known locally as the Coconut Wreck.

Cornelia Soule

Built: 1885 Sunk: April 26, 1902
Previous names: None Depth: 20 feet
Gross tonnage: 306 Dimensions: 123' x 31' x 10'
Type of vessel: Wooden hulled, 3-masted schooner
Builder: Miner & Son, Madison, Connecticut
Owner: C. Barry Power: Sail
Port of registry: New London, Connecticut
Cause of sinking: Ran aground
Location: Two miles west southwest of Rockaway Point Station

On April 26, 1902, Captain Bernet and five deck hands left New York City aboard the small coastal schooner *Cornelia Soule*, bound for Freeport with $150 worth of coal. No sooner had the short voyage begun when stiff weather forced the captain to change his mind about completing the voyage within the time schedule planned. Loathe to lose the distance he had already gained, he decided to wait out the storm at anchor, apparently unaware that the schooner lay on her hawsers in close proximity to the Rockaway shoals. Complicating the situation was the storm which, instead of abating, grew steadily worse, until his position became untenable. Two Life-Saving Stations were involved in the rescue: Rockaway Point and Rockaway.

Details in the Life-Saving Service report on the vessel's loss are wanting to the point of exasperation, with the life-savers' heroism and dedication taken for granted. "Wind blowing a SSW gale, weather foggy, and sea running high. The station lookout sighted and reported her at 1 p.m., and the keeper, expecting her to go ashore, had the beach apparatus transported to the shore. As the tide ebbed she fell into the trough of the sea and began to pound the bottom, and at 5:30 p.m. the master hoisted a signal of distress. The surfboat had meantime been brought to the scene, but it was impossible to board in such a sea, and the schooner lay nearly a mile offshore, too far for working the beach apparatus. In response to a call the keeper and crew of Rockaway station arrived and aided in the work. The life-savers built a beacon fire and stood by for a favorable opportunity to save the imperiled crew. During the night the wrecked craft began to break up, and at 3:30 a.m. the life-savers succeeded in launching the surf-boat and rescued the crew of six, landing them safe on the beach. The shipwrecked men were cared for at the station, and supplied with needed clothing from the stores of the Women's National Relief Association." Elsewhere, given strictly as a matter of statistics of the number of seamen saved, the Life-Saving Service records stated that the *Cornelia Soule* contained three men, not six.

The remains of the *Cornelia Soule* have not been positively identified, but a wreck in 20 feet of water at loran coordinates 26954.7 and 43759.1 could very well be what is left of the coastal schooner.

Cornelia Soule. (Courtesy of the Long Island Maritime Museum.)

Louis V. Place

Built: 1890 Sunk: February 8, 1895
Previous names: None Depth: Unknown
Gross tonnage: 735 Dimensions: 163' x 36' x 13'
Type of vessel: Wooden-hulled, 3-masted schooner
Builder: G. Christensen, Kennebunk, Maine
Owner: C.B. Parsons Power: Sail
Port of registry: New York, NY
Cause of sinking: Ran aground
Location: 1/8 mile east of Lone Hill Life-Saving Station

One of the most heroic episodes in the history of the United States Life-Saving Service was occasioned by the grounding of the schooner *Louis V. Place.* So extraordinary were the efforts of the life-savers that a detailed account of the event was written for the Service's annual report. I can do no greater justice to the dramatic events of yesteryear than to quote the report in its entirety.

"Stormy and extremely cold weather prevailed on the Atlantic Coasts from Florida to New England during the 7th, 8th, and 9th of February, 1895. On the morning of the 7th the storm center was in the vicinity of Charleston, South Carolina, and twenty-four hours later it was off the coast of Massachusetts, with marked increase of intensity. The temperature in Florida on that morning (February 8) was the lowest ever recorded there by the United States Weather Bureau, while in New York City it stood at zero. Wind velocities were also very extraordinary, as high as seventy-two miles an hour having been reported at Woods Hole, sixty-eight at Block Island, and fifty-three at Sandy Hook, and snow fell during the 7th and 8th all along the coast from North Carolina to Canada. During the four days from the 6th to the 9th, inclusive, there were casualties within the scope of the Life-Saving Service to twenty-nine vessels of various descriptions, carrying crews aggregating one hundred and twenty-nine men, from none of which were any lives lost, with the exception of the schooner *Louis V. Place*, which was wrecked in the morning of the 8th on the coast of Long Island, (Third District,) between the Blue Point and Lone Hill life-saving stations.

"The *Place* was a three-masted schooner of seven hundred and thirty-five tons measurement, built in 1890 at Kennebunk, Maine, hailing from New York, and carrying a crew of eight men, including the master and mate. It appears from the testimony of the survivors that she sailed from Baltimore, Maryland, under the command of Captain William Squires, on Monday, the 28th of January, bound for New York City, laden with one thousand and one hundred tons of coal, and passed out of the capes at the mouth of Chesapeake Bay about 10 o'clock in the forenoon of the following Monday, February 4th, having the wind fresh from the west-southwest. The weather, though crisp, was clear, but the water was rough, and soon after the schooner cleared the capes the wind veered to north-northwest, blowing hard, and the sky became overcast with thick clouds. All the light canvas was furled and the vessel stood on her course during the rest of the day and succeeding night under her lower sails only. On the next morning, Tuesday, the 5th, the gale had increased to such force that the sails were reefed down, with the exception of the foresail, which was so stiff with ice that the sailors could not handle it. The air at that time was biting cold and the rigging, sails, and entire hull of the vessel gathered ice to such a degree that she was kept under control with much difficulty. She was held to her course, however, as well as possible throughout the day and following night until the next morning, February 6th, when the severity of the weather had somewhat abated, permitting the reefs to be shaken out of the sails and the ice to be beaten off, so that she was able to make considerable better progress up the coast.

"On the morning of Thursday, the 7th, however, the gale shifted to the northeast, blowing with great violence, and the weather became very thick. The sails were reefed again, and the schooner labored heavily along until 2 o'clock in the morning of the 8th, when the tempest hauled to the westward, raging with greater fury than ever, and causing a wild and very dangerous cross sea. The crew had now been subjected to four days and nights of bitter exposure, and their arduous duties had allowed them so little rest that they were not only well nigh worn out, but almost disheartened.

"At this time the position of the *Place* was wholly a matter of conjecture, but Captain Squires is said by the survivors to have believed that he was not far off Sandy Hook. By 7 o'clock his vessel was little better than a drifting iceberg—almost wholly unmanageable, her running gear frozen in the blocks, her sails as stiff as boards, and her deck sheeted with ice. The atmosphere was so thick that objects could not be discerned at any considerable distance, and at about 8 o'clock the captain, totally bewildered as to his bearings, but confident that he could not be far from land, cast the lead, which showed about eight fathoms of water, whereupon, although his ship was leaking freely, he concluded to drop his anchors and try to ride out the storm. Calling aft the crew he informed them of his purpose, gave each a ration of liquor, and urged them to move about as

Louis V. Place. (From the author's collection.)

rapidly as possible. They did the best they could in their weak and miserable condition but all their feeble efforts to clear away the ice-bound anchors failed, and the master then instructed them to put on all the clothing they could wear and remain upon the after part of the vessel. An attempt to change the course would have been futile, and therefore none was made, but all the halyards were cut away in order that the sails might run down if they would, and the progress of the vessel toward the land be somewhat stayed. They were, however, so rigid with ice that they stood almost as upright in their places as before, and, as there was nothing more that could be done, the now thoroughly discouraged men gave over and simply awaited the dreadful fate they could have no doubt was close at hand. Not more than ten minutes afterward they heard the ominous breakers ahead, and a few minutes later the schooner lay pounding on the bar, the seas coming over every inch of her hull, and the crew flying to the rigging for their lives.

"About five minutes before stranding she was discovered by Surfman Saunders of the Lone Hill crew, who was on the beach, and ran at once to the station, where he telephoned for the assistance of the crews of the two adjacent stations, Point of Woods on the west and Blue Point on the east, and then dispatched a messenger to the eastward to notify his own keeper and crew, who were absent on attendance at the wreck of the four-masted schooner *John B. Manning*, which had stranded some hours earlier about halfway between the Lone Hill and Blue Point stations. The crews of both these stations had started out early for this wreck, and although their routes were beset with the utmost difficulties incident to an ugly winter storm, they succeeded in reaching the *Manning* in good time to rescue every man on board, nine in number.

"When their work was completed and they set out to return to their respective stations, they were all considerably fatigued, and several of them were frost-bitten. The Lone Hill crew found that to haul their beach apparatus back was beyond their strength, and, therefore, leaving it behind, they began to retrace their difficult journey under additional adverse condition that the cutting blasts of the gale, at a temperature of only three or four degrees above zero, were directly in their faces, blowing at a rate ranging from an average of over thirty to a maximum of upward of fifty miles an hour, and laden with blinding snow. On their way they were met with the information that a three-masted schooner was stranded near their station, and that their presence there was urgently needed. Hurrying on with all possible speed they soon reached the wreck. Meantime the other two crews above-mentioned had received the appeal for aid sent by Saunders over the telephone, and promptly responded. The Point of Woods crew, traveling from the westward, with the gale at their backs, were quickly on the ground, having with them their Lyle gun and other beach apparatus, while the Blue Point crew, coming the other way, arrived somewhat later. While on their homeward journey from the *Manning* they were intercepted by a surfman from their station conveying the news of the wreck to the westward, and at once facing about they bent their steps in that direction, picking up abreast of the *Manning* the abandoned Lyle gun of the Lone Hill crew, and dragging it along with them on a sled.

"The stranded vessel lay between three and four hundred yards from the beach, about one-eighth of a mile eastward of the Lone Hill Station, the surf was sweeping her from end to end, and her crew were to be seen in the port mizzen rigging at intervals when the atmosphere was not obscured by the frequent squalls of snow—three standing in the shrouds just above the sheer pole, two higher up, one still higher, standing on the ratlines between the crosstrees, and two on the crosstrees themselves. The tide was at flood, the surf very heavy, filled with a grinding mass of porridge ice two feet in depth, and the gale was at the climax of its fury, while the beach was strewn with great cakes of ice piled in some places to the height of six or eight feet.

Under these circumstances no human power cold put a boat afloat, or, if that had been possible, propel it through the angry sea of broken ice that heaved and surged between the shore and the wreck. There was one means only by which the imperiled men could possibly be saved, and that was the breeches buoy apparatus, which the life-saving crews prepared to put in operation without delay. Just as they were placing the Lyle gun in position for firing, two of the men standing a little distance above the sheer pole, where the waves constantly drenched them, who subsequently proved to be the captain and the cook, were observed to fall into the sea and disappear. This appalling spectacle, so early in the awful tragedy, gave evidence that the shipwrecked crew must have already lost much of their vitality, and excited grave apprehension that more of them would be lost even should no unusual difficulties arise to impede the operations necessary to effect a rescue.

"Scarcely had the poor fellows fallen from their places when the gun was fired and the projectile flew over the wreck, landing the shot line across the foretopmast stay, whence it slipped to the jib boom, too far away from the sailors to admit of expectation that they could possible get it, and therefore without delay the gun was fired a second time. This shot laid the line across the spring stay between the fore and main masts, the bight of it falling down and swinging almost within grasp of the shipwrecked men. The people on shore devoutly hoped that this line, apparently obtainable without serious difficulty, might prove to be the means of a speedy rescue, and much anxiety and disappointment were experienced when it was observed that no movement was made to reach it. The life-savers, however, allowed it to remain where it was, in view of a possibility that the sailors might by some means ultimately secure it, and meanwhile as soon as practicable fired a third shot which landed its line fairly across the main topmast stay. Still, the shipwrecked people continued to maintain their places in the mizzen rigging without a sign of a movement to get possession of the all-important line upon which, as far as could then be known, their lives depended.

"The weather had continued squally during these operations, often shutting out the vessel from view, and therefore considerable time had necessarily been consumed. It was then about 1 o'clock, and there were a few moments of clear sky, which afforded a chance to send out a fourth shot. This, however, did not fall aboard the vessel, and before anything further could be done the weather again closed in thick with falling snow that effectually concealed the *Place* from sight for the space of almost three hours. When it again became possible to see her the painful fact was disclosed that there were only four men left in the rigging, two of the six last seen having perished and fallen overboard during the squall. These proved to be Gustave Joeby (or Gaiby), the mate, and Charles Allen, who had charge of the donkey engine. The gun was now fired for a fifth time, and laid the line across the wreck, but before its exact location could be determined snow set in again and nothing could be seen. The short winter day was now almost gone, and the men stood earnestly on the alert to fire once more the instant the wreck should be visible. In a few minutes the coveted opportunity came, and upon its first sign the sixth shot went out, landing the line across the fore-topmast stay. There was yet sufficient daylight for the life-saving men to perceive that the persons on the wreck did not stir. Darkness was at hand, and with its coming disappeared all reasonable hope of effecting a rescue with the breeches buoy before morning. The night was wild and intensely cold. It would be little less than a marvel if any of the poor fellows should survive its awful terrors, and the watchers huddled on the beach by the beacon fire maintained their anxious vigil with unwavering fidelity, praying for some favorable change of conditions, ever so slight, that might warrant an attempt, however desperate, to launch a boat. But none occurred.

"When daylight broke, almost twenty-four hours

had elapsed since the stranding, and there were apparently only two living men left on the wreck. The third of the four who had been seen at the close of the previous day, August Olsen, was near the two survivors in the crosstrees, frozen to death, while the body of the fourth, Fritz Oscar Mohr, hung in the rigging head downward, held by the lashings he had placed about himself, swaying to and fro at the merciless sport of the gale.

"The survivors subsequently stated that Olsen was too weak to crawl around the mast under the shelter of the topsail, which they had cut adrift and drawn around them when they first went aloft, and that they could not help him. He was, therefore, compelled to remain where he was, wholly unprotected from the storm, and perished there about 2 o'clock in the morning. Mohr had lashed himself to the shrouds soon after the vessel stranded, and the exact hour of his death could not be determined. At sunrise the Lyle gun was fired once more, throwing the shot line across the main topmast stay, whence it swung to the mizzen rigging, very near the two sailors visible there, and the life-savers, praying that the men might secure it, and firmly believing that they would if they had yet sufficient strength, left it where it was. Still, no movement was manifest, and an almost despairing effort was quickly made to throw one even nearer to them. this shot was too high, and passed above the mizzen topmast, falling clear of the vessel. Without delay the ninth and last of the series was fired, laying its line fairly across the hull, between the main and fore masts. The tide was so low at this time that the rail was not submerged, and one of the men on the crosstrees descended, and, standing on the rail, made an attempt to haul off the line, but finding himself unable to do so abandoned the effort and crept feebly part way up the mizzen rigging. The life-saving men made signals to him to take the line aloft so that his shipmate might help to haul it off, but he paid no heed. It was now 3 P.M. of the second day, and hope was fast slipping away from all hearts. As a last resort the whip line was unbent from the shot line, and the breeches buoy was attached to the latter, when signals were made for the men to haul away, the idea being entertained that they might possibly make themselves fast to the buoy and be drawn ashore by that means. But the signals received no answer. It was plain that the sailors were too nearly exhausted to afford any aid in their own behalf, and at last all thought of making a rescue with the breeches buoy was abandoned. Of the nine shots fired only two failed to place the line fairly on board, while most of them had been landed where, under only a little less desperate conditions, they might have been readily secured.

"The breakers soon began to comb over the hull again, and signals were made for the sailor in the shrouds to join his shipmate in the crosstrees, where he would be somewhat sheltered by the topsail. The boat was taken from the wagon to the edge of the surf, and again and again driven as far as human power could force it into the ice-laden breakers, only to be spitefully hurled back upon the shore. Dangerous and almost hopeless as was the task, each succeeding failure only more and more sternly impressed the men with the dreadful extremity of the shipwrecked sailors, each succeeding effort was made with even more desperate energy than the preceding one. The last attempt

Coated with ice. (Courtesy of the Long Island Maritime Museum.)

of the afternoon took place at sunset, but the gathering darkness called no halt to the unconquerable purpose of the devoted life-savers, who now withdrew their boat a little way from the water and rested, only to renew their wasted powers and then push out again the instant a ray of hope should appear. Impatiently waiting and watching for the first sign of a feasible opportunity, none appeared until close to midnight. Then the tide was receding and the surf had fallen a little, while the wind was somewhat less powerful, and the masses of ice not quite so dense. Once more all hands stood by to make a launch. Forty hours had elapsed since the vessel stranded, and it was now or never for the perishing men on the storm-swept hulk. Every man of the life-saving crews realized full well that the supreme moment was at hand. At last, with one mighty rush they sent the boat afloat, Keeper Baker of the Lone Hill Station at the helm, and Keeper Rorke of Blue Point, with five other fearless fellows, at the oars. The waves ran high and the heavy ice pounded the boat with great fury, but her resolute crew drove her onward with all the strength at their command, and before many minutes laid her safely alongside the wreck. Aroused by the shouts of the life-savers that deliverance was at hand, the poor fellows in the crosstrees cautiously crept out and slowly descended the shrouds to the rail, whence they were helped into the surfboat. Two of their shipmates hung in the rigging, but they were dead, and the situation was too perilous to recover their bodies at that time.

"The boat had already suffered considerable injury from the incessant heavy blows of the ice, and Keeper Baker wisely determined to lose no time in getting the rescued men ashore. The powerful set of the eastward current considerably retarded the shoreward progress and carried the boat about a quarter of a mile east of the starting point, where it was pulled to the beach without disaster but not without additional serious damage. Between 12.30 and 1 o'clock A.M. on the 10th the rescued men were taken into the station, where for the first time their pitiful condition was fully revealed. William Stevens, the stronger of the two, was badly frozen about the face, ears, neck, hands, and feet, but his condition was far less wretched than that of his shipmate, Soren J. Nelson, whose feet were frozen almost solid in his boots and who was little more than barely alive. Their clothing was removed and their frozen limbs were bathed in snow, cold water, and linseed oil, and then properly bandaged. Stimulants were administered to accelerate circulation, and they were carefully placed in warm beds, where they lay under the watchful eyes of the surfmen throughout the remainder of the night. During their protracted imprisonment of more than a day and a half in the crosstrees these two men, cramped in position and penetrated to the marrow by the piercing cold, maintained their existence only by the exercise of the most courageous and persistent self-control. Not daring to sleep for a single instant, and unable to move more than a few inches, they kept awake and preserved sufficient circulation in their bodies to sustain life only by shaking and severely pounding each other, while by turns, as their moods alternated, the temporarily more sanguine one would encourage his despondent companion with strong words of hop or admonition. Stevens was of much the more tenacious temperament, and no doubt the rough usage visited by him upon the body, and even the face, of his shipmate largely contributed to save the latter's life.

"About 9.30 in the morning Lieutenant Maguire, the inspector of stations in the Third Life-Saving District, reached Lone Hill bringing with him Dr. Overton, of Patchogue, who at once took medical charge of the sailors, and a half hour later Dr. Robinson, of Sayville, for whom the keeper had telephoned an hour or two before, arrived and cordially cooperated with Dr. Overton. The wounds of the men were carefully dressed, proper medicines administered to them, and on the next day, at their own desire and by the advice of the physicians, they were sent to the marine hospital on

Staten Island. Nelson's feet were so grievously frozen that he was necessarily carried on a stretcher. Information has since been received that the amputation of both feet was found to be necessary, and after lingering until the 2d of March the poor fellow died of tetanus."

The bodies of August Olsen and Fritz Oscar Mohr, the two men lashed to the rigging, were taken ashore, and, after a coroner's inquest, transferred to Patchogue for burial. The same disposition was subsequently made of the body of Gustave Joeby, (or Gaiby,) the mate, which washed on to the beach near the Forge River Station, fifteen or twenty miles to the eastward. A burial lot was generously donated by Mrs. Augusta Weeks of Patchogue, where the three bodies were reverently interred with appropriate ceremonies. On the 22d of February the body of Captain Squires was rescued from the surf by men of the Life-Saving Service, between the Shinnecock and Southampton stations, and the next day was given in charge of his brother, A.P. Squires of Good Ground. On the 26th the body of Charles Allen, the engineer, was found one-half mile west of the Moriches Station, and on the following day was committed to the custody of the coroner. No tidings have ever been received that the body of the cook has been recovered. He was said by one of the survivors to be a Norwegian, but neither of them knew his name.

"It is most profoundly to be deplored that all on board the *Place* could not be saved, but the credit due to life-saving crews is in no way diminished. They faithfully stood to their duty and accomplished all that human power could effect. Fourteen out of twenty-one, notwithstanding their necessary activity, were frost-bitten, several were for a number of days barely able to keep about, and one, whose ears and face were very badly frozen, was so seriously disabled that after all was over he lost consciousness and had to be removed to his home."

On February 13, the *John B. Manning* was pulled off the bar by wreckers and returned to service, but the *Louis V. Place* was beaten to pieces where she lay.

Marjory Brown

Built: 1889 Sunk: October 20, 1913
Previous names: None Depth: Unknown
Gross tonnage: 1,211 Dimensions: 198' x 40' x 17'
Type of vessel: Wooden-hull 4-masted schooner
Builder: Jackson & Sharp Company, Wilmington, Delaware Power: Sail
Owner: S.K.J. Thompson
Port of registry: Perth Amboy, New Jersey
Cause of sinking: Foundered
Location: Off Montauk

The story of the loss of the *Marjory Brown* was made all the more dramatic by a remarkable sequence of photographs which show the schooner's actual demise only minutes after the fortunate crew abandoned ship. According to Captain Joseph Walker, master of the *Marjory Brown*, "After battling with a gale all Monday night, the weather became thick and foggy, and I discovered that the heavy seas had started the seams of the schooner. By 4 o'clock on Tuesday morning there was five feet of water in the hold, and by 8 o'clock this had increased to thirteen feet. The pumps would not work and we were helpless. After stocking the long boat with provisions, we were about to cast off when the smoke of a steamer was seen in the distance. We made signals of distress and then got into our boat and pulled away from the schooner to the *Berlin*, where we were treated with every kindness."

Walker's matter-of-fact portrayal of events evokes none of the dread or trepidation which must have been felt by the captain and crew as they overcame the awful adversity of abandoning ship in mountainous seas. Perhaps seamen take such an undertaking in stride, but the landlubber is left with a thirst for more particulars of how the abandonment was conducted. Yet the facts remain nearly as simplistic as Captain Walker stated them.

The *Marjory Brown* was en route from Newport News, Virginia to Providence, Rhode Island when she began to leak. She was carrying 2,000 tons of soft coal. It is likely that coal dust clogged the pumps and rendered them useless.

The North German Lloyd steamship *Berlin* was bound from Naples and other ports in the Mediterranean to New York City when she happened across the foundering schooner off Montauk, at 10:09 a.m. on October 20, 1913. She hove to in order to lend assistance. C.W. Ward happened to have a camera on board and quickly snapped five photographs. A slower shutter finger would have missed all the action, because only a few minutes passed between the first picture and the last.

The *Berlin* took the six survivors to Hoboken, where they arrived none the worse for their experience. It was just another day in the life of a sailor.

This is an actual photograph that was published in *Marine Review*. The photographer was C.W. Ward. Note the lifeboat to the right, off the stern of the *Marjory Brown*.

Panther

Built: 1870 Sunk: August 24, 1893
Previous names: None Depth: Unknown
Gross tonnage: 712 Dimensions: 190' x 36' x 13'
Type of vessel: Iron-hulled ocean-going tug
Power: Single cylinder steam engine
Builder: Reaney, Son, & Archabold, Chester, Pennsylvania
Owner: Philadelphia & Reading Railroad Company
Port of registry: Philadelphia, Pennsylvania
Cause of sinking: Foundered
Location: Two miles off Southampton, Long Island

For twenty-three years the steam tug *Panther* led a dull and onerous career towing barges along the East Coast. For the most part she was engaged in the coaling trade, transporting fossil rock from Philadelphia to ports in New England. Then came 1893 and a couple of storms, the second of which she did not survive.

The first gale of 1893 in which the *Panther* was caught occurred in February. She left Philadelphia on Sunday the 18th with the barge *Reliance* in tow, headed for Newburyport, Massachusetts. As tug and tow were rounding Montauk they encountered a terrible gale. "All of the steamer's sails were blown away and the houses stove. About 8 o'clock Monday morning the wind increased to a hurricane, and both steamer and barge labored heavily. The steamer was hove to in an endeavor to keep her head up to the wind. In so doing the barge's hawser drifted under the steamer's stern, and to prevent its getting afoul of the propeller it became necessary to cut the hawser and set the barge adrift. The hurricane was then blowing from the west, with a fearful sea.

"The barge was lost sight of in the blinding snowstorm soon after the hawser was cut. The *Panther* succeeded in getting up under Long Island last night when the gale veered to northwest and moderated. The steamer is iced up badly. The *Reliance* has since been reported lost on Block Island, with Capt. Remington, her crew of three, and the Captain's wife. The finding of a doll on the beach at Block Island gave rise to the belief that Capt. Remington's child had been lost, but the child is safe at Somerville, Mass."

Six months after the catastrophe in which five lives were lost under such tragic circumstances, the *Panther* encountered another storm on route to Newburyport from Philadelphia. The tug had on board a crew of sixteen men and 739 tons of coal; she was towing the barge *Lykens Valley*, which was carrying four men and nearly 1,500 tons of coal.

On the third day from port the *Panther* approached Sandy Hook under conditions from which meek captains fled. Storm warnings were posted, but Captain George Pierson, master of the *Panther*, thought he could reach his destination before the predicted storm arrived. He turned the tug eastward and plowed through mounting seas along the south shore of Long Island. The night of August 23 found tug and tow being overtaken by adverse weather which was steadily growing worse.

According to a contemporary account, "The wind, which was blowing from the northwest, was not very strong at first, but it soon gained in force. Even when the storm was comparatively mild the *Panther* found it impossible to keep her bow straight or her tow in position. As each minute passed the strength of the storm increased until it was blowing a regular hurricane, and the *Panther* found herself at its mercy."

The most graphic and detailed account of the *Panther's* last moments came from one of the survivors, Edwin Cummings, a fireman. "Toward nightfall we began to ship heavy seas, and the barge especially got a terrible drubbing. The storm increased in fury during the night, and at 6 o'clock on Thursday morning it was something terrible. All of us knew we were in great danger. At 6:30 the mainsail went by the board. All hands went to work to rig up another sail abaft the smoke-stack, and this staid for a while. Several of the crew now wanted the Captain to put into Sandy Hook Bay, but he refused to do so. About 7 o'clock I was raking up one of the fires, when a frightful sea struck us and smashed in the engine house.

"I heard the Chief sing out, 'Oh, my God, we're done for now!' The room was filled with steam and I groped my way up on deck. Another fireman, Eli Jeffries, whom we called 'Pop,' was thrown back into the fire-room and badly hurt, but he scrambled on deck. As the boat was becoming unmanageable, we set to work to unbend our fore staysail, and tried to nail it over the broken side of the engine house so that we might keep them going. The wind, however, kept tearing the sail into ribbons.

"Then the Captain determined to cut loose from the barge, and we headed more out to sea, thinking if we kept her head to the sea the tug might ride out the gale. After we had all climbed into the rigging the seas kept coming mountain high, sweeping clean over the boat. It took the men off the rigging like flies. The mate and myself were way up in the mainmast rigging, he to lee-ward and I to windward.

From *The Illustration American.*

"We saw every other man aboard go over. In the last batch, taken off by an awful sea, were four – two of the seamen, the Chief Engineer, and the lamp trimmer. The Captain had long since been carried away. This left the mate and myself the only living souls aboard. He said to me: 'Cummings, my lad, keep cool, it's our turn next. Perhaps we'll get to shore, but we've got to take chances. Keep cool my boy.'

"A huge roller broke over us and took him off just then. The waves fell on me again and again as if there were a hundred ropes pulling at every limb in my body. My wrist, as I hung with one hand only, was terribly strained. I knew I couldn't hold on much longer, and when the next sea smashed over us, I had to let go. The next thing I knew, when I shook myself in the water, the mate was close by me, swimming. We were about twenty fathoms away from the tug, and when we were lifted on the top of each wave we could see her main-mast, and even notice her settling. The mate sung out:

" 'We'll make it all right,' as near as I could understand him, and then he was carried out of sight.

"I saw Billy Daly and the little mess boy. They were swimming with planks across their chests. I then got hold of the top of the pilot house, which had been washed away, and floated on this for a long time. It suddenly turned over, and I remember no more till I came to ashore in the hands of my kind friends here."

The "here" to which Cummings referred was the Southampton Life-Saving Station. According to the Life-Saving Service report, "Between 7 and 8 o'clock in the morning, steamer foundered 2 miles offshore. The weather was so thick and rainy that the vessels could not be seen from the land. Three of the *Panther's* crew drifted to the beach in an unconscious condition, supported by life-preservers and wreckage. Life-saving crew and others went into the heavy surf and, endangered by the floating wreckage, assisted to rescue the above-mentioned persons and to resuscitate them, providing one with clothing from the station supply. All the rest were drowned, as well as those on the *Lykens Val-*

ley, which stranded soon after she was abandoned by the *Panther* and at once went to pieces, no persons being at any time visible on board. Sixteen (all but one) of the bodies of those lost from both vessels were subsequently recovered by this crew and crews of Mecox, Georgica, and Amagansett stations, and were given proper burial."

From assistant engineer Albert Smith we get another description of the frightful ordeal. "In the trough of the sea we were turned over, first a forward somersault and then a backward, and we would go under the water and then we would be tilted up again to an awful height. We turned twice every time we were in the trough. We could talk to each other once in a while. We were half a mile off shore when I saw the last of the captain. A sea bigger than any we had had come, and we fell from it together. I was under water so long that my courage gave out. I said to myself: 'It's no use; I may as well end it by opening my mouth.' That moment I came up. I looked for the captain and he was nowhere to be seen. Probably the sea tore off his life preserver and that ended him."

The only other survivor was able seaman Victor England, a Russian Finn who barely spoke English.

Also lost in the same storm were the schooner *Empire State* and all ten of her crew, two men of the crew of the *Chocura*, four men of the crew of the *Mary F. Kelly*,, and the captain of the *Hinckley*. Other sailing ships were driven ashore, and most of those that managed to limp into port afloat were dismasted or had their sails blown to tatters or suffered extensive damage to their upper works. The coasts of New York and New Jersey were severely battered by wind and waves. Roofs were blown off hotels and cottages in seaside resort areas, and flooding destroyed many roads and properties.

The wreck of the *Panther* has yet to be identified among the many carcasses that litter the ocean bottom off Long Island.

Books by the Author

The Popular Dive Guide Series

Shipwrecks of Massachusetts: North
Shipwrecks of Massachusetts: South
Shipwrecks of Rhode Island and Connecticut
Shipwrecks of New York
Shipwrecks of New Jersey (1988)
Shipwrecks of New Jersey: North
Shipwrecks of New Jersey: Central
Shipwrecks of New Jersey: South
Shipwrecks of Delaware and Maryland (1990 Edition)
Shipwrecks of Delaware and Maryland (2002 Edition)
Shipwrecks of Virginia
Shipwrecks of North Carolina: Diamond Shoals North
Shipwrecks of North Carolina: Hatteras Inlet South
Shipwrecks of South Carolina and Georgia

Shipwreck and Nautical History

Andrea Doria: Dive to an Era
Deep, Dark, and Dangerous: Adventures and Reflections on the Andrea Doria
Great Lakes Shipwrecks: a Photographic Odyssey
The Fuhrer's U-boats in American Waters
Ironclad Legacy: Battles of the USS Monitor
The Lusitania Controversies (Book One): *Atrocity of War and a Wreck-Diving History*
The Lusitania Controversies (Book Two): *Dangerous Descents into Shipwrecks and Law*
The Nautical Cyclopedia
Shadow Divers Exposed: the Real Saga of the U-869
Shipwreck Heresies
The Shipwreck Research Handbook
Shipwreck Sagas
Stolen Heritage: Grand Theft of Hamilton and Scourge
Track of the Gray Wolf
USS San Diego: the Last Armored Cruiser
Wreck Diving Adventures

Dive Training

Primary Wreck Diving Guide
Advanced Wreck Diving Guide
Ultimate Wreck Diving Guide
The Advanced Wreck Diving Handbook
The Technical Diving Handbook

Nonfiction

Wilderness Canoeing

Science Fiction

A Different Universe
A Different Dimension
A Different Continuum
Entropy (a novel of conceptual breakthrough)
A Journey to the Center of the Earth
The Mold
Return to Mars
Silent Autumn
The Time Dragons Trilogy
- *A Time for Dragons*
- *Dragons Past*
- *No Future for Dragons*

Sci-Fi Action/Adventure Novels

Memory Lane
Mind Set
The Peking Papers

Supernatural Horror Novel

The Lurking: Curse of the Jersey Devil

Vietnam Novel

Lonely Conflict

Videotape or DVD

The Battle for the USS Monitor

Visit the GGP website for availability of titles:
http://www.ggentile.com

THE LUSITANIA CONTROVERSIES

THE TWO-VOLUME HISTORY OF WRECK-DIVING

There is more to a book than its title. There is the subtitle. A subtitle is an explanatory device which describes the topic of a book more fully than its title. A case in point is *The Lusitania Controversies*. At first glance the title implies the sole subject of the *Lusitania*. But each of the two volumes possesses a subtitle which explains in greater detail the global premise of which the *Lusitania* is but a part.

Together, both volumes present the entire history of wreck-diving, from its meager beginnings in the 1950's to the advent of technical diving in the 1990's.

Book One is subtitled *Atrocity of War and a Wreck-Diving History*. One quarter of the volume is devoted to the construction, career, sinking, and aftermath of the *Lusitania*. Three quarters are devoted to the history of wreck-diving and to autobiographical experiences of the author, who became an essential element in wreck-diving and a pioneer in technical diving. Coverage extends to 1979, and includes a section on the author's first *Doria* trip, in 1974.

Book Two is subtitled *Dangerous Descents into Shipwrecks and Law*. This volume continues the history of wreck-diving from 1980; describes numerous dives on ever-deeper shipwrecks; a number of incredible penetrations into the vast interior of the *Andrea Doria*, including the recovery of two bodies; and details the beginning of mixed-gas diving to the point at which an expedition to the *Lusitania* became practical. The volume concludes with a detailed description of the 1994 *Lusitania* expedition (of which the author was a part) and subsequent legal activities.

The two volumes are larger than the sum of their parts. They comprise biographical content with incredible underwater adventures: some hair-raising, others deadly, all exciting: a fascinating excursion into the real world of wreck-diving and the evolution of the activity.

www.ingramcontent.com/pod-product-compliance
Lightning Source LLC
La Vergne TN
LVHW010055110826
845155LV00028B/342

* 9 7 8 1 8 8 3 0 5 6 3 4 6 *